DRIVING YOUR SELF-DISCOVERY:

A Pocket Guide for Understanding & Leveraging Coaching

Christine Haskell, Ph.D.

Run for Cover Publishing, LLC

SEATTLE

Driving Your Self-Discovery: A Pocket Guide for Understanding and Leveraging Coaching

© 2021 Christine Haskell

ISBN: 978-1-7329081-0-9

EBOOK ISBN: 978-1-7329081-1-6

Cover design, interior design and illustrations: Rob Nance

For information about special discounts for bulk purchases, please visit: www.runforcoverpress.com

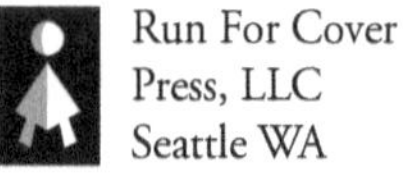

Run For Cover
Press, LLC
Seattle WA

Contents

Contents

Introduction

Coaching is one of the most valuable developments of the last century for advancing an individual's effectiveness. Until a few years ago, it was an expensive development tool exclusive to the c-suite.

Over the last twenty-five years, coaching has become more accessible and affordable. Coaching provides an exceptional tool to raise our levels of awareness and attunement. It improves our relationships and assists us in discovering our potential. Coaching helps us cultivate a hospitable inner environment for learning in our professional lives to achieve more significant results—*that's* why organizations have made it more and more available.

Organizations recognize that keeping an open mind amidst ever-increasing pace of crisis and competition is a struggle, but necessary for creative problem-solving and effective management. And, they understand that being a learner takes practice and commitment.

Psychology, with its focus on an individual's potential for growth and maturity, and philosophy with its emphasis on critical thinking, lay the groundwork for coaching. Because coaching borrows heavily from other disciplines like psychology, philosophy, neuroscience, and other related fields, questions inevitably arise: What is coaching, really?

The most common idea coaches state upfront with a client is that coaching has distinct boundaries with psychotherapy practices. Because of this, it is deeply misunderstood, mischaracterized, and practiced by a vast spectrum of talent, creating doubt in the marketplace. Coaching is rarely described well, and its voice seldom heard with enough clarity.

This little pocket guide attempts to explain how I personally interpret and practice coaching. It describes how coaching leverages basic principles from psychology, in particular, the difference between dipping and dwelling in the past; what the needs are in all of us to which it serves; the methods by which it addresses these needs; and, what outcome of a coaching intervention could ideally be.

The book suggests my central belief that coaching, with someone well-trained, is one of the single most significant steps any of us can take towards greater awareness and fulfillment. Investing in coaching can reduce anger and frustration, defeatism, poor confidence, and general feelings of being lost or stuck while helping you achieve results.

This guide is an overview of the purpose and meaning of coaching. Use this guide to help you consider the qualities you want in a coach; prepare for a coaching engagement; think of the kind of issues you might bring to coaching for discussion. You can also use this guide to stimulate your own reflective practice.

COACHING V THERAPY

Executive coaching is very solution focused. Some engagements can be as short as 1-3 sessions. Other clients need more extended periods, from six months to a year. All engagements utilize tools and strategies to interweave results and relationships at the individual, team, or organizational level. It sounds like a simple concept, but it is not easy to pull off. A coach's background varies, accounting for a broad spectrum of talent in the marketplace. A coach can hold a behavioral, social science, or psychology master's or doctoral degree. And, there are also coaches practicing with little professional background or educational foundation. Both types of coaches submit to the requirements of an accredited coaching program and take an exam. In addition to certification requirements, some coaches further increase their dedication to rigor, investing in academic degrees and managerial experience. As of the writing of this book, there are no state licenses for coaching.

Psychotherapy generally is a long-term process. A patient works with a therapist to diagnose and resolve problematic beliefs, behaviors, relationship issues, feelings, and sometimes physical responses generally resulting from past trauma. The therapist holds a clinical master's or doctoral degree and submits to state licensing requirements. In general, states license two specific types of roles—mental health counselors and marriage and family therapists.

In choosing a practitioner with coaching or therapy, the client needs to decide what level of rigor they are looking to engage with and distinguish for themselves the difference between wise counsel that might be transformative versus friendly advice less likely to cause a meaningful shift.

Dipping V Dwelling

Both therapy and coaching are collaborative processes based on the relationship between an individual and a practitioner. Both are grounded in dialogue, and provide a supportive environment allowing clients to talk openly with someone objective, neutral, and nonjudgmental.

Both practitioners use a client's past as a tool for understanding present behaviors. It is here a therapist will *dwell to heal*, and a coach will *dip to frame understanding* of how the past influences the present. Coaching can be therapeutic, but it is not therapy. Together with the client, both practitioners will work to identify and change the thought and behavior patterns that are keeping clients from feeling and performing their best.

While there is a shared understanding and rigor between trained therapists and coaches educated on behavioral theory, the fundamentals of coaching are what distinguish it from therapy. Therapy dwells in the past and attempts to heal an individual's emotional pain by reversing the suppression of memories and emotions. Coaching dips into the past, helping an individual frame painful experiences or challenges to increase awareness of past patterns and understanding of their impact in present situations. In this way, coaching is not therapy, but it can be therapeutic.

> *Coaching focuses on helping leaders work through their dilemmas so they can truly learn on the job (in front of others, under pressure) and directly translate that knowledge into results for their teams and, ultimately, the organization.*

Coaches use diagnostics to assess individual and organizational effectiveness and performance. They do not diagnose mental illness. A coach with a background in behavioral science, psychology, or a related field has an understanding of the fundamentals of human behavior from a theoretical perspective (how family systems work, social development, adult learning, our lopsided natures, and the impact of denial—to list a few things). Therapists apply a similar lens and use it to determine illnesses and pathologies so their patients can be clinically treated.

The coach's focus is typically present-forward compared to the retrospective lens of the therapist. The coach does not focus on healing the past but instead takes note of how it influences the present and what strategies can help the client increase their effectiveness. Coaching never requires medication, micro-dosing, coordination or services, or adjunct therapies though the client might opt for any those experiences separately with a therapist.

Chapter Reflections

What outstanding questions do you have about coaching?

____

____

____

What qualities mentioned in this section would you like to seek in the coach you work with?

____

____

____

What have you learned that you didn't know before about the difference between therapy and coaching?

____

____

____

HOW FRAMING THE PAST PRODUCES INSIGHTS

Here we will look at some of the fundamentals of psychology—specifically how family systems work, our lopsided natures, and the impact of denial—understanding these ideas sheds a little light on concepts used in personal and professional development.

Gaining awareness of past hurt can promote insight and healing. Understanding our past informs our present possibilities, helping us link awareness to action and goals.

Families Are The Factories Where People Are Made

Here we will look at some of the fundamentals of psychology—specifically how family systems work, our lopsided natures, and the impact of denial—understanding these ideas sheds a little light on concepts used in personal and professional development.

Gaining awareness of past hurt can promote insight and healing. Understanding our past informs our present possibilities, helping us link awareness to action and goals.

The roots of our need for seeking support lie deep in our pasts. They are often imprinted within our families. It does not matter how much effort we invest in our development. Somewhere in childhood, our path towards emotional maturity has almost certainly been hampered. Even if we came from a loving family, no one leaves youth unscathed. Everyone has some deep psychological injury from their past—what psychology refers to as a 'primal wound.'

We could blame time. Compared to other animals, *Homo sapiens* have an exceedingly long, structurally claustrophobic processing time. A giraffe can stand up minutes after it is born. By the age of sixteen, a human will have spent around 50,000 hours in proximity to its parents. A female salmon mother will choose a site, dig a nest with her tail, deposit 100s of eggs, and then swim away without seeing a single one them again. Even the African elephant, the largest land animal on the planet, is sexually mature and independent by the age of ten.

But humans dawdle and delay in their development. It's a year before we take our first steps and two before we can think and speak coherent thoughts. It takes close to two decades before we are recognized as adults—and we are currently pushing those boundaries further. Twenty years is a long time to be influenced by such a highly irregular, distorting organization we call home, and it is even more distinctive supervisors, our parents. If parents are our first supervisors, of sorts, this incubative style of learning translates to the organizations we serve, where we seek mentors and teachers for every major milestone—becoming a manager, increasing our scope, running a division, or becoming a senior leader. And, consciously or unconsciously we choose people who fit the same model from those we have experienced in the past.

Families are the factories where people are made. Over many long summers and winters, we learn how to scan and assess an environment for nurturing, safety, and success. We are intimately shaped by the ways and manners of the significant people around us. We tune into their frequency. We log their likes and dislikes and their favorite expressions so we can anticipate their habits. We know how they will respond to interruption and delay. We are sensitive to their tone when they're irritated. We know the atmosphere of

"

**Families are
the factories
where people
are made.**

our home in the early spring morning as we wait to go to school and, in the evening, as we prepare for dinner. We memorize the textures of the wallpaper and the smell of fresh laundry coming out of the dryer. As adults, we can still recall the taste of certain foods we had at birthdays and know intimately the tiny sounds a parent made while reconciling the weekly checkbook. We might return home for a holiday as adults and learn—despite our jobs, responsibilities, and aching bodies—that we are seven again. We take these hyper-awareness skills into the workplace and observe our managers and key stakeholders—those with a hand in our professional destiny—with the same scrutiny, and adapt our behaviors accordingly. We adopt certain roles in their presence that can limit our opportunities.

During our elongated development, we are at first, in a physical sense, completely at the mercy of our caregivers. In many ways, we are so frail. The shadows under our bed are out to get us in our sleep. We need help crossing the road. We develop complex strategies for tying our shoes and putting on a winter coat. We need direction writing our name. Once in the workplace, we watch our backs for the potential deception of others. We find the line between permission and forgiveness. And in some cases, as we learn to take a stand on issues we care about, we defer to the highest rank in the room rather than assert our innate authority, startled by our developing inner voice.

As children, we are also exposed emotionally. We are not equipped to understand who we are and won't be for some time. We don't know where our feelings come from; why we are sad or what makes us furious. We don't understand how adults fit into the bigger picture or why they behave as they do. We take what the big people around us say as truth; we can't help but exaggerate their role on the planet. Our survival depends on it. We are entangled in their attitudes, ambitions, fears and predispositions. In this way, our upbringing is always particular and peculiar. Unchecked feelings in the workplace render us immediately vulnerable. Unsure of our path, our definitions of success still in flux (or worse, defined by others), we try to sort out the risks and safety features of the organizational climate in which we are trying to survive. Figures in our midst—managers, mentors, adversaries, stakeholders—are all bigger than life until we can sort them safely into categories.

As children, we are unable to let the inertia and force of those around us roll off our backs. Without a hard shell of our own, we absorb it all. If a parent shouts at us, it shakes us to our core. We cannot tell that some of their harsh words were not really for us necessarily, that their cause might have been a difficult day at work, or are the aftershocks of their own childhood; it is like an all-powerful, all knowing giant has decided, for good (if unknown) reasons, that we are to be defeated. Everything is all or nothing. In the workplace, this manifests as highly reactionary behavior. We approach a sensitive topic in a meeting and notice everyone's demeanor shift—were we just set up? Someone failed to recognize our efforts and contribution—are we being edged out of the group?

It is also hard for us to reckon with a parent's disappearance, when they travel or relocate, that they didn't leave us because we did something wrong or because we are unworthy of their love, but because even adults aren't always in control of their own destinies. Likewise when major shifts in leadership occur, there are some who wish they had done more or said more on that leader's behalf, thinking their actions might have changed the outcome.

If parents are having a heated discussion, we think they must hate one another. To children, a conversation with raised voices (throw in a slammed door, some swear words, and screeching tires out of the driveway) may feel catastrophic. It's like everything safe is at risk of collapsing. In that kind of climate, there is no understanding from the child's perspective that disagreements are normal part of relationships. They do not understand that a couple may be committed to a life-long union while also wishing that the other go to hell. How we experience parental conflict—whether we engage as peacemaker, take sides, or shut down altogether—is often how we behave in the presence of organizational strife. Knowing what is motivating our behavior when we are under pressure might save us from intervening at the wrong time.

Children are equally vulnerable to their parents' beliefs. They can't parse why they should not mix with another family from school. There is no logic why they should follow dress codes or choose one religion over another. They don't feel as passionately about why they should wash their hands as often as they do or be early for school. All of these 'isms' represent a partial understanding of priorities and reality to which they must subscribe because their parents do. Same with organizational behaviors and practices. With which teams do we collaborate best? Which people or teams do we shun? With which norms do we comply and which do we ignore?

Childhood has a fixed radius from which there is little ability to escape. There is no other place for us to be like school or a job. Under the supervision of our parents, we start to develop a social network. Even when things are going well, we are in an open prison—probably why we flex our boundaries by flirting with the idea of running away. In organizations we cultivate friendships and develop networks. There are above ground networks that everyone can see, and underground networks that contribute to how work gets done, and not everyone is included.

As a result of the idiosyncrasies experienced in our early years, we develop distorted views and unbalanced narratives about ourselves. The family template is established. Without awareness, we will live and relive in that template in whatever group we encounter for the rest of our lives because our brains like to match patterns. Parts of our internal makeup start to develop in odd directions. Perhaps we can't easily trust. Maybe we become unusually scared or unusually engaged around people who raise their voices. We might not believe compliments we are given, can't tolerate being touched, or become irritable engaging in small talk. We seek familiar templates and patterns and we want to repeat or repair those patterns. If we had an overbearing mother, we might seek overbearing friends, partners, or bosses. Or we might go to great lengths to avoid them entirely. If our organization has made an impression on us, had a strong culture in which we had to contort ourselves in order to fit in, we work hard to stitch our family and organizational templates together. Sometimes they map, sometimes they do not. In either case, there is learning to be had.

Regardless, our response to people who are overbearing will be imbalanced. We don't need to have suffered something shocking, illegal, evil or malicious for those distortions to develop. The causes of our wound do not have to be outwardly remarkable, but their impact can often be significant and long-lasting. Some people can survive abusive parents who suffered from addictions and turn out more resilient than another person who survived a schoolyard bully and a distant father. That is how fragile childhood is—remarkable incidents aren't the only ones that are liable to cause our wires to cross. The same is true to bosses, mentors or key people in our professional careers. Some people leave bruises and yet those very same actions might not impact another employee in quite the same way.

Lopsidedness

Experiences we have from childhood leave us lopsided in our reactions—likely to overreact or overcorrect depending on the stimulus. We are too shy or too bold, too firm or too accepting, too focused on getting to the top or infuriatingly apathetic. We are obsessively eager to succeed or painfully wary and nervous in the face of our desires. We are naive or pessimistic. We shrink from taking a chance or run toward risk with wild abandon. We are fixed in our belief that going it alone is wisest or are desperate for another to complete us. We are in white-hot pursuit of knowledge or impervious to new ideas.

The spectrum of lopsidedness comes in many shades, and more are always being added. What is known is that these lopsided behaviors come at an enormous cost. They leave us less likely to make the most of our opportunities, less able to create or find satisfying lives, and generally, make us less fun to be around socially or professionally.

Because we are reluctant scholars of our emotional histories, we conclude that our lopsided nature is something we cannot change—that they are fixed. "This is just how I am," we think. I am controlling, or don't get my satisfaction out of work I get it from my family, or I am not good with people, or don't trust my peers, or not good at office politics. These stories we hold about ourselves are not initially adaptable or up for consideration.

The truth is that things are much more hopeful. While challenging to us in the short term, lopsidedness (by its very definition) is, in fact, able to be brought into balance. Our lopsidedness is in response to something specific that happened in the past. We are a certain way (controlling, not good with people, not trusting, and so forth) because a primal wound knocked us off a more fulfilling course years ago. Having to contend with a competitive parent, we took refuge in underachievement or extreme overachievement. Dealing with a parent disgusted by their body might have made them hypercritical, making it hard for us to be seen or noticed, and attention became frightening or hard to negotiate. Being forced to reckon with financial instability, we had to overachieve professionally, seeking economic and social gains. In the face of a distant or dismissive parent, we fell into patterns of emotional avoidance and reactive violence. An explosive parent might have moved us toward extreme shyness and aversion to attention or limelight. Constant hovering when we were young could have encouraged nervousness and, around any complex and intense situation, abject panic. A continually busy, distracted parent might have planted the seeds for energy-draining, attention-seeking look-at-what-I-did-or-learned-today behaviors as an adult.

"

We are reluctant scholars of our emotional histories...

There is a logic to our lopsidedness if we look to our histories. In the presence of conflict—dismissiveness, explosiveness, hovering, inattentiveness—a trigger was established. A way of thinking developed because of how we coped when we were children. And this isn't meant to be harsh, but our lopsidedness enables a way of being that trends toward immaturity—they take us in the opposite direction in which we mean to move, sabotaging our progress. Our first reactions, therefore, are never our fault. They are merely the remnants of our younger selves' attempt to deal with something beyond our capability—at that time.

When a child suffers at the hands of an adult, they absorb the result as a reflection of something that must be wrong with them. They think they are not enough. If someone humiliates, ignores, or hurts them, it must be because they are stupid, unacceptable, and worth abandoning. It can take many years, and much patient inner examination, to understand the truth: that the hurt was undeserved. As adults, we learn the importance of context: many other things were going on- and off-stage, in the parent's interior life for which the child was innocent. But that doesn't stop us from internalizing a boss's gruffness or anger (at something) as something we may have caused or contributed to.

Also, because children cannot leave the big people whom they relied upon and were vulnerable to, children succumb to a deep longing to fix the broken person they clung to for security. Children often conclude that they must fix all anger, addiction, or sadness of the grown-up they love. They aim to please. It could take decades of inner exploratory work to determine that we might feel sad about, but are not eternally responsible for, those we cannot change—and even longer to decide, perhaps, to move on. These behaviors can show up later as co-dependent relationships where one person constantly prods or helps another in their job to the point where they are instilling a learned helplessness. Or, a real need or yearning for co-workers to step in to help, step in or speak up when some infraction occurs—yet they never do, cultivating resentment and frustration.

"

There is a logic to our lopsidedness if we look to our histories.

Similar childhood legacies plague communication patterns. When something is wrong, children have no language or logic to understand the cause. They lack confidence, self-management, and verbal skill to get their points across calmly and with authority. Children err on the side of overreactions: begging, insisting whining, exploding, screaming. Or, conversely, to excessive under-reactions: moping, resentment, silence, avoidance. It might not be until middle age that we start to shed those initial reactions of screaming or sulking from those who misread our needs and more carefully and calmly try to explain them instead.

Another less desirable quality of the family template is that it provokes large-scale generalizations about how people operate. Just as those early experiences unbalance us, so do our heuristics. We don't live life in generalities; we live our lives in the particulars. Our wound was formed in highly individualized contexts. One particular adult incessantly picked on one particular family member or shouted at their particular partner late at night in one particular three-story house in one particular main road through town. Or the wound may have been caused by one specific parent who responded with fear and disbelief, followed by intense contempt after one specific job loss from one specific company. But these scenarios give rise to expectations of other people and of life more broadly like the partners we choose or the bosses from whom we accept job offers. Over time, we expect that everyone will become violent, sooner or later. We think that every partner will turn on us eventually. Every boss will use us as a steppingstone or sell us out when it counts. We assume that every money problem will unleash a deep depression and then disgust for the other person. The character traits and mentalities that were formed in response to one or two central actors of childhood become our templates for interpreting pretty much anyone, and using those templates prohibits our ability to see alternatives. For example, the reliability, focus, and determination to succeed at any task that we evolved to keep a profoundly depressed and angry mother engaged becomes our second nature. Even when she is no longer present in our lives, we remain individuals who need to shine at every meeting, who require a partner to be continually focused on us, and who cannot listen to negative or discouraging information of any kind. In these situations, we are both in the past and the present. When we work our template with others and test our sense of the particulars for a given situation, we stand in the doorway of the present peering through a narrow keyhole at the drama of the past. Without awareness of this dynamic, we both watch and re-enact that drama over and over.

A child in the presence of parents that fight, for example, can carry that experience well into adulthood. One outcome of that could be a desire to avoid conflict altogether. While the original cause of our avoidance is no longer in the picture, it can carry a heavy price.

Dealing with our lopsidedness can be thorny because we don't always know why we have our quirks or how they came to be. Sometimes we explain them away as not affecting us. We think that marital affair happened between our parents. It did not occur to us. As a result, we might not acknowledge these events as having any significance in our minds. Yet, we can't explain why we run away from a boss who is looking out for us to a more abusive manager. We don't understand why small things that shouldn't impact us infuriate us. We might get defensive or adopt a laissez-faire attitude with success believing in the end that it was never really ours to have. Because the meaning behind our reactions remains hidden, we miss out on benefiting from significant sources of possible sympathy. Meaning, if we lack the context for why we react the way we do, so does everyone else because we are judged by the behavior and decisions our wounds inspire, not on the wounds themselves.

The hurt we experienced might have started by being let down by a parent or bullied by a peer, but today we show up as a micromanager or demand a kind of loyalty from our teams that crosses a line. It might have started with a competitive mother. Maybe a father had an affair and left the family. It could have been a peer we looked up to or made ourselves vulnerable to and who later betrayed us. Today, it manifests as shyness, inability to make decisions, or take a firm stand.

Ultimately, driving self-awareness through coaching comes down to us, and a desire to make our lives easier. Without it, we find our paths are tougher than they should be because of the beliefs we hold that people are incompetent, mean, and unreliable rather than (as is usually the case) fellow wounded soldiers of what we have all traveled through, a complicated early history.

Denial, Blocked, And Stuck

Our interpretations of childhood experiences are the single most significant cause of how we function emotionally as adults. Therefore, what is surprising and unfortunate is how little of the past we can remember—even our recent past. We can recall the basic facts and a few occurrences here and there. Still, in terms of grasping detail with camera-like precision, how our present influences us by our interpretation of the figures and events of our early years, we are often beginners or naturally skeptical as to the point of examining the past. In many cases, we willingly block these accounts.

The tendency, and sometimes desire, to forget the primal wound of childhood is not hard to understand. To be presently impacted by events so far into our past feels implausible and crushing, but also humiliating. To subscribe to the notion that our personalities might remain forged by incidents from before our sixth or seventh birthday leaves us feeling helpless. No amount of blunt ("just get over it," "let it go"), or cliched-sounding mental health determinism ("think positive," "reach out to more people") denies our hopes for a more dignified life of adult autonomy. We want to make sense of our moods in terms of what is happening in the present. If we feel angry with someone, we would like to believe the cause lies with them and their actions rather than something tripping a low-lying frequency laid four decades ago, rendering us especially sensitive and flinty.

Over time the lens on the past softens. What was a challenging norm becomes an endearing exception or quirk. Our perspective is aided by family photos, almost always capturing happier moments, even if staged. There is much more likely to be an image of one's mother going down a playground slide with a carefree expression than of her yelling at her children about the misery of everything she gave up for her current predicament. There will be a shot of one's father genially posing with the children or family friends in very on-trend plaid pants, but no visual record of his long, brutal mealtime silences. Much mental editing goes on, encouraged by all participants, anything to be remembered as a softer version of themselves. The same mental editing happens in the workplace as we recall situations where we, trying to get ahead or advance our agenda, spun up rumors about another person. Or the time we made a new acquaintance that might make a good mentor, then quickly ghosted them without explanation, yet we only remember what was important to us in those scenarios. We remember those rumors as merely trifling or recall not thinking enough of our need of another's help to respect them enough to follow through. We recast and rationalize our behavior so we feel better, not necessarily considering the impact we had on others.

As we age, we lose the idiosyncratic and peculiar perspective of a child and instead view the world through the pragmatism of an adult. An adult's observation of a toddler's tantrum in a bookstore is judged as frustrating, dramatic, and bad-tempered. That one perspective has merit. At the same time, it might be harder for us to access support or empathy and attempt to recreate the strange inner world of a small person (an inner world we once had). The child might feel tired, confused, and exasperated that naptime is so far away. For him, admitting that he's tired is admitting defeat. He might be lonely and shy by being the smallest person in a large store with beige carpet and books that have no dragons in them. He is far from his teddy bear, left by mistake in the car outside. As we age, we judge heightened reactivity as "emotional." People who lead with their emotions can be judged as frustrating, dramatic, or irritable. We will proceed with caution, unsure what we will

"

Over time the lens on the past softens. What was a challenging norm becomes an endearing exception or quirk.

encounter, or find ourselves watching our words around them. Without seeking to understand the reason for their reactivity, we think they are volatile.

When an adult locks the door to the spare bedroom to ensure silence for an hour-long business call, we don't typically picture the scene from the perspective of the young child on the other side. For them, this repeated exclusion may seem proof that everything magical and joyful has suddenly gone. Or when the parent has after-hours obligations that help raise her profile at work, and she misses opportunities to support after school activities. Or when the parent is incessantly on his phone, laptop or another gadget—checking in on it like a digital pet—ignoring the needs of the small child seeking connection in the here and now. Adults' professional responsibilities are no small thing; they maintain a livelihood and enable opportunities for each family member. At the same time, these slights to our self-worth and self-esteem, if too numerous, have a cumulative effect. It becomes difficult for us to keep in mind how much in our respective personalities was marked by what are (from a grown-up perspective) almost laughably minor yet hugely potent incidents. We see this same distraction among leaders in a meeting and assume what we have to say must not be important enough for them to pay attention to. Management could be tending to a major issue, but we may feel the lack of support in this moment and because it is so familiar to us, conclude that we, in fact, are not working on the highest priority issues if management can't tear themselves away from their phone during a one-on-one meeting, a large group check-in, or all hands meeting.

It is not merely that we have forgotten the past. We could, in theory, re-enter the mental spaces we once occupied. We have our reasons for pushing aside or ignoring the memories and willfully limiting reflection on our histories.

We maintain a safe distance from our inner selves because of what we might learn about ourselves, or the people that hurt us will likely be uncomfortable. We might discover that we were angry with and resentful about certain people we were only meant to rely upon—or worse yet, that we misdirected our anger toward innocent people trying to protect us. We might discover how much ground there was to feel intensely anxious, inadequate, and guilty on account of the many errors and misjudgments we have made. We might come to find out just how much happiness was nauseatingly compromised by our assumptions. This insight illustrates to us what changes we might consider about our relationships and careers. Faced with needing to take responsibility for our current outcomes, we have more choices about the future we want to have.

> It is part of the human tragedy that, as such creative beings we are such natural self-decievers of our unique greatness

Instead, we hide. It is part of the human tragedy that, as such creative beings, we are such natural self-deceivers of our unique greatness. We have many methods for camouflage, and we do much to escape being noticed.

We become addicted to the kind of numbness that comes from opting out. We float above the surface of life. Our addiction isn't to drugs or liquor (although that can happen too), but to the mundane, everyday activities that keep us busy, distracted, and exactly where we are. We watch television or clean the house, exercising or continually start new projects at home or work. We might cook or can food at odd hours or reorganize the garage.

We tell ourselves we are productive. To the world, it might even look that way, but our compulsiveness has motives. We watch the television to focus on news or narratives to avoid learning news and narratives about ourselves. We take on projects around the house or raise our hands for new projects at work to avoid losing ourselves in something of greater impact because with impact comes responsibility. As much as we crave meaningful work, we run from it. Addiction is not about what someone does; it's that they do what they do to avoid feeling what they feel and knowing what they know about themselves. We are addicts whenever we develop a twitchy reliance on something—anything—to keep us from encountering the angry dogs locked in the basement of our minds.

We lie to ourselves first, and later others, by being overly optimistic and cheerful. There is a fine line between optimism and happiness that is hard to detect. Optimism doesn't contain any remorse. It is insistent and upbeat, aggressive even in its persistence, but doesn't necessarily lead to fulfillment. Optimism can't tolerate any other emotion, especially sadness. So negative emotions are left unexplored to the point where they have the power to overwhelm us with disappointment, helplessness, and grief.

We lie to ourselves first, and later others, by going on the offensive. We attack and demean what we love, virtually guaranteeing we don't get what we genuinely want. We let go of the people we once wanted or even had as friends. We watch the careers we hoped one day to have pass us by. Lives we wanted to match and learn from fade into a fog in our consciousness. To prevent ourselves from feeling the loss of what we might never achieve, we begin to allow our goals erode.

We lie to ourselves first, and later others, by embracing cynicism and calling it pragmatism. We are preventing, we believe, future misery and disappointment. To preserve our dignity, we tell ourselves that all humans are terrible, and every activity is likely to fail so that the specific cause of our hurt does not attract examination and feelings of humiliation.

We lie to ourselves first, and later others, by filling our minds with lofty ideas, putting our intellect on full display in such a way that suggests we have little left to learn. Here, we stunt what development our personalities may require to continue to evolve.

We write dense books on big topics. We earn advanced degrees.

We seek positions on boards. Our minds are crammed with eso-teric information—facts perhaps most interesting at cocktail par-ties and dinner conversation. But we don't remember much about our own lives. We forget how things really were, back in the old house, when dad lost his spark, mom stopped smiling, our sibling started exhibiting anxious behaviors, and our ability to trust in happiness broke into tiny pieces. We forget because we might be repeating that very same pattern.

We acquire and share knowledge and seek new ideas that garner respect but also protect us against the essential knowledge from our emotional past. That knowledge that, if left untended, might attempt to interfere in our path: that knowledge that bubbles up at inopportune times threatening us to wake up. We bury our sensitive, personal stories like a time capsule beneath a mountain of knowledge and skills. We judge the possibility of a profoundly significant and intimate inquiry as weak, frivolous, and incon-sequential compared with an allegedly more impressive task of securing an executive for an important meeting or addressing a conference.

We prop ourselves on the glamour of being knowledgeable, ensuring we won't become too knowledgeable about ourselves. We learn about anything outside of ourselves to avoid the pain of self-awareness and true wisdom.

We lie to ourselves first, and later others, by suggesting that people are just simple beings. We tell ourselves that too much psychology might be a little too much static and complexity. We think too much knowledge clouds the facts. We rely on a version of robust common sense, denying ourselves a deeper connection with our awkward complexity. We imply that not thinking very much is evidence of a superior kind of intelligence and elevated emotional state—when it is the blankness of ignorance and lack of deeper thinking or curiosity leading to one-dimensional problem solving and a lack of creativity.

When we are with others, people who will judge us, we vigorously ridicule more complex perspectives on human nature. We discount personal investigation as unduly fancy, bizarre, or weird. The very desire to lift the lid on our inner life could never yield anything of value or goodness. This kind of sprightly self-ordering is most likely at the start of the week. We feel our most pragmatic at 9 am on a Monday morning as we muster our aggressive optimism toward our SMART goals. But this energy eventually softens in the late evening. We are confronted—sometimes harshly, sometimes by surprise—with more complex insights. Sometimes they come at once: the choices we have made, the impact we have had on others, and lost opportunities for happiness and contentment come into relief for the first or perhaps the umpteenth time. They pour through the nighttime window toward us as we stare into the moonlight. With an attitude of forceful common sense, we strive to make our moments of radical discontent seem like outliers rather than anchoring moments of insight they might be.

We want to believe that our personalities are non-tragic, simple, and easily understood so that we can reject the stranger, but more useful, facts of our authentic, more complicated selves.

Being honest with oneself and others has nothing to do with morality or righteousness. Seeing reality and ourselves with greater clarity is actively listening to a cautionary tale. We all could use much more of the truth because we pay too high a price for our believing our own lies. Our self-deceptions cut us off from possibilities of growth, creativity, and deep learning. Unused, our minds can evolve to being more argumentative and defensive, while others around us have to suffer our touchiness, pessimism, artificial happiness or defensive rationalizations. Neglecting our awkwardness buckles our very being, manifesting as insomnia or impotence, weight loss or gain, stuttering or depression, revenge for all the thoughts we have been so careful not to have. Self-awareness and increased self-knowledge are not luxuries. They are preconditions for sanity and inner contentment.

The Emotionally Healthy Childhood

An emotionally healthy childhood can't be idiosyncratic, dependent on a particular environment, or come down to good luck. With optimal development in mind, we can observe distinct themes that start to form a map. From there, we can see with greater clarity when we are taking a left turn, what we have to be grateful for, and where we feel our greatest shame. At a societal level, this map might serve as general guidance toward success, and a more emotionally stable and therefore slightly saner world.

An emotionally healthy childhood could give us the following:

A model for a lifelong advocate. Someone will put themselves profoundly at our service. When we were small and dependent, there was a person (to whom we owe our lives) who pushed their needs aside for a time to focus wholly on our own. If we have even a measure of mental health as adults, it is undoubtedly because of this advocate. They understood our babble and heard us into speech. They gave us their best guesses on treatment when we were sick. They calmed our fears, consoled us in our insecurities, and protected us from harm. They provided a protective barrier from the chaos of the world, showing us just enough of it—carving up experiences for us in manageable pieces. Without thanks or sympathy, they didn't expect us to ask how their day went or how well they slept. They catered to our needs so that we would, later on, be able to submit to the rigors and slights of daily life. This lopsided relationship was temporary. Modeling with consistency, they made certain our ability to form a healthy bond.

We generally think of egocentricity as a quality resulting from too much love or attention. But the opposite is true. An adult who is egocentric never got their fill as a child. Self-centeredness must have a clean run in the early years if it isn't to haunt and ruin the later ones. Those we regard as narcissists are unfortunate people who never got the chance to be exceedingly admired at the start.

In an emotionally healthy childhood, our advocate is there to give

"

With optimal development in mind, we can observe distinct themes that start to form a map.

us the benefit of the doubt. They offer us a positive spin on our behavior. We are judged on our potential in the future, not by what we are right now. From this, we learn kindness and charity.

If our advocate is a harsh critic, for example, they might say that we were 'attention-seeking.' Instead, they imagine that what we most need is a hug and some encouraging words. For example, we might have acted meanly. Our advocate contends that we must have been feeling threatened. If we dropped something accidentally or were negligent, our advocate remembers that fatigue could have explained it, or we were distracted by a new visitor.

Our advocate continually searches for the story behind the story. They look under the surface for more compassionate explanations. They help us to be on our own side. They help us to like ourselves. If we like ourselves, we learn not to be too defensive about our flaws. We learn there is always something to work on, constructively, and we learn to accept ourselves as we are.

In a healthy childhood, the relationship with our advocate is stable, dependable and long-term. We have faith they will be there tomorrow and the day after. They aren't explosive or fragile. They are almost boringly predictable—so much so, we might start to take them for granted. As a result, we project this trust in other relationships we develop throughout our life. We can believe that what has gone well once can go well again. This belief influences our choice of friends, adult partners, bosses—everyone. We aren't fascinated by people who are abrupt with us or unreliable; we don't relish being punished, judged, or mistreated. We can pick out influences who are kind and nurturing and don't view them as weak or deficient for being so.

If trouble strikes with our kindly partners, we don't go into an instant panic. We don't immediately try to defend ourselves by turning away, avoiding or cutting them off. We can confidently set about trying to repair a love or connection we know we deserve.

In a healthy childhood, we aren't always required to be wholly

"

Our advocate continually searches for the story behind the story. They look under the surface for more compassionate explanations. They help us to be on our own side.

good. We are allowed our emotions. We can get angry and some-times be disgusting. We can allow ourselves to feel tremendous sadness and disappointment. We can say 'no more, absolutely not, no way' when we disagree or settle a dispute with 'because I feel like it.' Our advocates are adults and know that we all, no matter what our age, have our flaws. As a result, they do not expect us to be fundamentally better than they are. We do not have to comply at every turn to be merely tolerated. We can let others see our shadow sides.

This kind of freedom within our family systems prepares us one day to submit to the demands of society without having to rebel in unproductive, self-defeating ways (rebels being, at their core, people who have had to obey too much too early). We can toe the line when it's in our long-term interest to do so. At the same time, we're not overly intimidated or indiscriminately obedient either. We learn to find a sound middle point, an emotional neutrali-ty, between being completely submissive and self-destructively defiant.

In a healthy childhood, our advocate isn't jealous or competitive with us. They can allow themselves to be overtaken and super-seded. They have had their moment in the spotlight, or else are having it elsewhere beyond the family. They can be proud rather than resentful of the achievements of the (usually same-sex) child. It doesn't need to be all about them.

The good advocate doesn't live through the child's accomplish-ments. They want them to do well, but for their own sake, and in their own way. There is no particular script that the child has to follow to be loved. For instance, the child doesn't need to become a doctor or a famous soccer player because that is the path their parent chose. The child isn't required to support their advocate's self-doubt or pump them up to others.

In a healthy childhood, the child learns that things that break can be fixed. Things that spill can easily be cleaned up. Plans can go awry, but new ones can be made. The advocate models for the child how to self-soothe, calm down, keep going, and remain hopeful. A voice of resilience, originally external, becomes the way the child learns to speak to themselves. They learn there are alternatives to panic.

Notably, even emotionally healthy childhoods suffer from things going wrong. No one has hung their reputation on the notion that anyone's childhood could ever be perfect. The advocate does not see it as their role to remove every frustration, pad every sharp corner, or remove every obstacle. They sense that much good can come from having the right, manageable kind of friction through which the child develops their own resources, coping mechanisms, and individuality.

> The advocate is neither entirely good nor wholly bad, and therefore is worthy of neither idealization or shunning.

Having contact with bearable disappointment, the child is prompted to create their own internal world. They can dream, generate new plans, learn to self-soothe, and build up their own resources.

The child can see that the advocate is neither entirely good nor wholly bad, and therefore is worthy of neither idealization or shunning. Just as the adult accepts the child with its faults, the child learns to accept the adult with theirs with a blend of melancholy, maturity, and gratitude. They learn that, like their advocate, they need to allow that everyone they come into contact with will be a mixture of positive and negative and that the presence of negativity or flaw is not a reason to shun. As adults, they won't fall quickly in love (becoming fast friends or lovers), nor will they become furious at the first moment of a let-down (by ghosting, shunning, or banishing). They have a realistic sense of what can be expected of life alongside another human who is, like them, good enough.

Unfortunately, despite all our advances in technology, education, and material resources, we are not much more advanced in the art of delivering emotionally healthy childhoods than previous generations. The number of breakdowns and inauthentic lives attempting to keep up with some external image of success shows no marked signs of decline. We are failing to offer one another tolerable childhoods not because we are malicious, apathetic, or uncaring. We are failing because we still have so far to go before we know how to do that most simple yet infinitely complicated of things: accept ourselves with emotional neutrality.

One tool that might get us there is coaching.

Markers Of Emotional Intelligence

Coaches with a background in psychology are grounded in family systems theory. They understand the impact a family template can have on adult development and how our lopsided natures can hold us back from making progress. They know how denial can lead to blocking learning and remaining stuck.

It is a great myth, and one that we have bought into, that we are one person at home and another at work. Now that we understand the basics of how families work, how our lopsided natures are formed, and how we become stuck, we have a greater sense of why emotionally intelligent leaders are so highly prized in the work environment. Maintaining an emotional equilibrium is conducive to increased creativity, better decision-making, and higher emotional intelligence.

One way to start understanding just how lopsided we have become from our earliest experiences is to identify a range of markers of emotional intelligence, visualizing how we rank in comparison. In therapy, we would direct most of our repair work and attention toward healing those early experiences that generated the most hurt and therefore contributed to the most significant gaps in our emotional health. In coaching, we recognize that these experiences occurred, gain awareness and insights about how they

"

It is a great myth, and one that we have bought into, that we are one person at home and another at work.

contribute to our present, and determine actions that will increase our effectiveness and performance.

At least five principles comprise emotional intelligence.

1. **Self-love: the ability to like oneself, wholly.**

   Before we can empathize with others' experiences, we must learn to understand our own internal experience—the emotional reactivity and interior monologue that is generated when we are under stress.

   Self-acceptance is the quality that determines how much we can be friends with ourselves, learn to become our own (caring) advocate, and commit to constructive choices that suggest we are on our own side. We must be able to demonstrate these behaviors not just when they are easy, but when it counts.

   When we observe a stranger pleasantly experiencing something we are not, how quickly do we feel less than or resentful? How long is it before we are questioning the fairness of things and making assumptions of how they came by those experiences? When another person irritates or demeans us in some way, can we let the grudge go? Can we see the action for what it was or are we left brooding and lose ourselves in overwhelming sadness, indirectly agreeing with the verdict of those judging us? Can we counterbalance the disapproval, neglect, or public opinion by the memory of the steady attention of a few stable, selfless, and significant people from our past?

   In relationships, do we have enough self-acceptance to leave an abusive partnership or boss? Or are we so down on ourselves that we carry an unspoken belief that mistreatment, disapproval, or outright abandonment is all we deserve? In a different vein, how good are we at apologizing to a lover, a family member, dear friend, or former colleague for things that actually might be our fault? How righteous do we need to be? Can we dare to admit mistakes, or does an admission of guilt or error bring us too close to a sense of complete insignificance?

How do we regard our desires? Therapy will venture into family histories and the bedroom for those answers. Coaches will look for historical patterns and the boardroom, seeking to understand how we define and self-edit our desires for success. Are our desires worthy or unworthy? Are we a little off, but not bad, since those aspirations originate from inside us, and we are not victims?

2. **Candor: the ability to be truthful and authentic about oneself.**

Candor is about being "real" when you might feel vulnerable to judgment and open in the face of difficult ideas and troubling facts. It determines the extent to which you can consciously open your mind, to thoughtfully explore and accept facts without denial—without lying to yourself (and then others).

One question both therapists and coaches get equally: "Am I normal? You've seen this before, right?"

The fact is, there is no normal. And, yes, we've seen it before.

The essence of candor is intimacy, with ourselves. How much can we admit to ourselves about who we are—even if, or especially when, the material is unflattering? How much do we need to insist on our own normality and sanity in order to accept ourselves and admit our inner natures? Can we explore our own minds? Can we confront "the angry dogs in the basement" of our minds? Can we shine light in those darker and more troubled corners without flinching too much? Can we admit to foolishness, envy, sadness, confusion, and galactic mistakes?

Around others, how ready are we to learn? This matters for parents and partners as much as it does for newly minted managers and CEOs. Do we need to take a criticism of one part of us as an attack on everything about us? How ready are we to listen when valuable lessons come, painfully, over and over again through multiple contexts?

3. **Social Skills: the ability to communicate, persuade, influence, and listen.**

   Can we patiently and reasonably put our disappointments into words that, more or less, enable others to see our point? Or do we internalize pain, act it out symbolically or discharge it with counterproductive rage?

   When other people upset us, do we feel we have the right to communicate or must we slam doors and retreat into sulks? When the desired response isn't forthcoming, do we ask others to guess what we have been too angrily panicked to spell out? Or can we have a plausible second go and take seriously the thought that others are not merely being nasty in misunderstanding us? Do we have the inner resources to teach rather than insist?

4. **Motivation: having an interest in learning and improving oneself.**

   Do we have the strength to keep going when there are obstacles in life? Motivation is about setting goals and following through with them.

   When something deeply interests us, we take initiative and demonstrate the commitment to complete a task. If we are truly passionate about our goal we will persist through adversity, boredom, and frustration and find creative ways through setbacks.

   Embracing better health, taking steps to advance our career, attending graduate school, saving for retirement, and paying

"

Around others, how ready are we to learn?

off loans are examples of goals that motivate us internally and result in self-improvement.

Marrying at the "right time", getting the best grades, having the latest gadget or car are examples of chasing goals that flaunt wealth or status and can represent a slippery slope. Failure in the face of these kinds of goals is unlikely to result in a constructive learning opportunity. More than likely failure to maintain the perfect house, keep the kids in private schools, avoid divorce and hide poor performance at work will result in increasing self-doubt, and reducing one's ability to be their own best advocate (and friend).

5. **Self-Management: the ability to control and manage our impulses and emotions under pressure.**

How do we react in the face of risk? And, how do we manage our impulses in relation to those risks? Do we think before we speak/react? Do we express ourselves appropriately?

How well would we perform a challenge in the form of a public speech, a romantic rejection, period of financial strain, immigrating to another country or lengthy physical illness? Sometimes a small cold can set us back in ways we didn't expect. How close are we, at any time, to financial, professional, or personal disaster? How much grit do we have?

Is the stranger or outsider dangerous or benevolent? If we lean towards being a little more direct than most, will they accept us or ghost us? Will unfamiliar situations end in a disaster? Around love, how tightly do we need to cling? If a lover, parent, sibling, friend is distant for a while, will they return? If a boss neglects regular touch points, stakeholders go silent, or direct reports fail to check in are they sabotaging us, or will they still support our efforts? How controlling do we need to be? Can we approach a stranger or colleague we don't know to connect on some common interest? Or move on from an unsatisfying relationship?

Overall, do we think the world is expansive, safe and rational enough for us to have a genuine shot at fulfillment, or must we settle, resentfully, for inauthenticity and misunderstanding?

Our first answers to these questions are not our fault, or anyone else's. They are merely the first responses that were wired into us during a galvanizing experience. Many of these questions are so hard to answer sincerely in a positive light. But, by considering them, we are at least starting to know what sort of impact our primal wounds have had and, therefore, what we need to do to address it.

Chapter Reflections

What past patterns might be impacting your present possibilities or ability in achieving your goals?

____

____

____

____

How does the concept of "lopsidedness" show up for or in you? What triggers can you identify that impact your performance with others?

____

____

____

____

What beliefs do you have about others that block you or keep you stuck?

____

____

____

____

What aspects of a healthy advocate resonated with you the most? Why?

____

____

____

____

What aspects of emotional intelligence do you think you need to work on most?

____

____

____

____

3

HOW COACHING CAN TEND TO THE PRESENT AND FUTURE

Now that we've reviewed some of the fundamentals of psychology—specifically how family systems work, our lopsided natures, and the impact of denial—it's important to underscore the stance of the practitioner you want to engage, and why you want to engage them. Chemistry and philosophical alignment matter when it comes to making progress.

A therapist will diagnose your lopsidedness, and dwell with you in reviewing past experiences to heal or help reduce your emotional pain. They do this by reversing the suppression of memories and emotions; by talking with you and getting you to talk.

Coaching *dips* into the past and attempts to help you frame your experiences in a way that provides insights about your present and future. Specifically, coaching helps you gain awareness of your*self* as an individual, how you influence and interact with teams, and how well you negotiate change.

It is here we come to a fork in the road and will focus exclusively on the practice and value of coaching.

Coaching is a tool; like all tools, it has been designed to help us overcome an innate weakness we came by naturally and to help us learn to nurture, augment, and extend our capabilities. Coaching earns distinction as a tool and intervention for its ability to inter-weave relationships with results.

"

While coaching can initially be focused on a single individual, coaches take a bi-focal view of their client within the context of their larger system.

It sounds like a simple concept. Those who have risen quickly know it is not easy to pull off.

Coaches claim a wide spectrum of specialties—from coaching skills for management, to building block skills from scientific literature, to a billion dollar self-help industry helping you figure out "what to do when you grow up"—and this book doesn't claim to cover such a broad range of topics.

Here, we take a flyover view of how executive coaches leverage principles from psychology, philosophy, neuroscience and other disciplines, and effectively model them with clients as they navigate their environment. Coaches search to find teachable moments when they will be able to *link being, doing, and learning with attaining actionable results*. In this way, clients leverage coaches as a true business partner helping them face distinct challenges in achieving results and gain clarity on what is hindering their progress.

While coaching can initially be focused on a single individual, coaches take a bi-focal view of their client within the context of their larger system. They look at the forces that shape and influence the client. Clients subconsciously react to the field in which they operate with their own emotional responses, which propel them forward or hold them back. Clients react within that field and this sets off a chain of reactivity around them. Coaches need to be able to see the how the system impacts their clients in order to see how their interventions succeed or fail. Without the systems perspective, coaches have limited impact.

Coaching has been devised to correct the otherwise substantial difficulties we face in understanding how we operate as individuals, our impact and influence on others, our ability to participate and lead high-performance teams. Done well, under pressure, in front of an audience—are all demonstrations of fully integrated skills such as self-love; radical candor; awareness of what motivates us and others; and self-management. To perform well under stress requires us to trust ourselves first, then others, and communicate successfully, honor our potential, while feeling adequately calm, confident, authentic, direct and unashamed.

For many of us, that is a tall order.

For such an important invention, coaching is still low on overt signs of innovation. Much of the training and information on the market has been updated and repackaged.

However, there is new emphasis on neuroscience, brain development, creativity, and consciousness. There is increasing interest in making coaching more readily available to all members of the organization. Technically speaking, it requires only a quiet room free of interruptions, fifty minutes, possibly twice a month, and some thoughtful conversation where both people are fully present. The level of training a coach grounded in psychology needs to undertake requires a period of extensive education in the workings of the mind, which – in more responsible institutions – has a similar cost, rigor, intellectual ambition and periods of hands-on experience as getting a pilot's license.

To deliver on its promises, coaching relies on distinct components. Here are four.

1. Results Driven

The outcomes a client is there to achieve should be the sole focus of a client engagement. To lose site of that is to waste the client's time, money, and energy. The organization needs the client to be as effective as possible on the goods or services that contribute to the organization's success. Coaching support that drive for results.

2. Partners on the journey

The coach stands shoulder-to-shoulder with the client in gaining personal and professional mastery. Together, they detangle and assess the issues, pressures, and problems they face. The coach observes, inquires, motivates and challenges the client to perform optimally.

3. **Engaged in the challenge**

   This process helps the client gain awareness and insights about what forces they might be succumbing to that take them off course, and what they avoid. In the confines of the coaching dynamic, the coach confronts and challenges the client on how they might be getting in their own way.

4. **Connects key concepts to gain insights**

   The coach makes the connection between behaviors to outcomes, keeping the leaders focused on outcomes but widening their lens on how to get there. This is an essential aspect of coaching where coaches help clients to understand which behaviors are linked to which business goals. It's important for the client to understand that they are not an island, and that the responsibility remains central to the leader achieving results through their behaviors with the team.

Key Principles Of Coaching

Components of being results-driven, a good thought partner, engaged in the challenge, and a connector of insights are important for an effective coaching engagement. *How* that is delivered requires certain qualities.

A few key principles fair better than long lists of models, worksheets, and tactics—no matter how road tested they are. We use the term *guiding principles* for a reason, because they literally *guide* us when we are overwhelmed by emotions that come up in stressful work situations, like anxiety, boredom, frustration, resentment, anger and disappointment. Guiding principles apply when things are going well, too, like joy, euphoria, excitement, enthusiasm, and happiness because *they dictate what we do next.* They guide us when we are under pressure and the stakes are high, like when our team doubles and our scope increase overnight and we are now responsible for teams in three geographic regions. Achieving

"

We use the term *guiding principles* for a reason, because they literally *guide* us when we are overwhelmed by emotions...

personal and professional mastery at *being, doing, and learning with attaining actionable results*—in front of others, when our career is on the line—is hard work.

Coaches use the following principles:

- Note their whole experience (both mind and body)

- Adopt a systems lens

- Use their own experience and a systems lens in their approach to coaching

Often referred to as "signature presence", "executive presence", or one's "whole self," it is really about understanding what is it about *that* coach that we can't get from any other.

Everyone has a unique presence that gives everyone else they come into contact with a particular experience they can't get anywhere else. This isn't to say that we can't be replaced, but at the same time, we are unique beings and have unique perspectives to offer. A coach should not be performing *techniques* on clients. No one likes that experience, and it's not helpful. A trainer, for example, who performs the same training in three cities is not a coach. They are giving a cookie-cutter experience to a high volume of people. I mentioned partnership as a key quality in coaching because it is a value I hold deeply. A coach is a sounding board, peer, and shoulder-to-shoulder collaborator presenting their unique perspectives on a client's most intimidating challenges. This requires the coach to be candid, *the ability to be truthful and authentic about oneself.*

The coaching relationship is built on trust, the ability to provide candid feedback, and a genuine presence. The coach's ability to be authentic helps elicit authenticity in the client. In this way, the coach helps the client bring their full self to their goals, challenges, and relationships crucial to their success.

"

A system is like a spider web, where the action of one person can impact the experience and potential reactions of everyone or thing else within that web.

Adopting A Systems Lens

A system is like a spider web, where the action of one person can impact the experience and potential reactions of everyone or thing else within that web. Coaches require a system lens to understand where their clients work. A systems view is by definition nonlinear. It enables the coach to spot patterns of interaction and interdependence within and across specific areas of the system

A coach looks at the system both inside-out and outside-in. At the center of the web is the leader and their personal work. This is where the coach and the client reflect on the client's values, motivations, goals, strengths, and core challenges. Next out is the client and their team(s), departments, vendors, customers, and strategic stakeholders or partners. The further area from the client is the market, the economy, the natural environment, and political shifts.

This last phase used to seem academic but is coming into the foreground now more than ever. When tariffs increase, whole revenue models need to be recalibrated as is the case with cars. When natural resources are recognized as finite, whole product lines and supply chains need to be reconsidered as is the case with the paper coffee cup. When a company is questioned about their ethics and their impact on elections, how people approach launching their service requires more rigor in thinking through unintended consequences—as is the case with social media services. All of these external factors (and more) impact how we go about our day to day business and how we feel about our work. And, how we feel about work impacts how content we are ourselves and how we treat others.

When the coach focuses too narrowly on the client (their goals, challenges, and inner difficulties), the whole ecosystem in which they function is lost. And the client is influencing and being influenced by the interrelationships of that system (their team, departments, vendors and customers) all the time. Also important is the global area in which they operate.

Combining Our Unique Experience And A Systems Lens With An Approach To Coaching

Combining the unique qualities the coach brings with a systems lens is what makes the application of the coaching method unique. Depending on how they've been trained and their professional experience, each coach will identify, emphasize and reflect something different from the systems in which we operate. This is one of the reasons we need to pay attention to what resonates with us when we choose a coach.

Coaching follows a predictable flow. First the coach and client *contract* on goals for the engagement. They *plan* how to achieve those goals by determining a roadmap. This determines how the coach *intervenes* with the client and what interventions the client will then practice. Together, they *debrief* on what progress occurred and what next steps the client should take. This is an action research approach seeking business results while building client capabilities to identify, practice, and review their skill development across multiple contexts.

While these steps appear linear, human reactivity and responsiveness are not. A client might be on the verge of landing a vision and mission with their team or organization when they reach out for coaching. Another might be planning a big change initiative. Those projects will continue forward without the coach's ability to influence it. The coach will instead focus on the heat and chaffing that arises in and between the individual, team, and larger ecosystem of the "systems web."

By linking the coach's whole experience with a systems perspective to the coaching approach, the coach brings ideas, particular filters and perspectives, and abilities to constructively challenge their clients. Coaches can take a strong stand in stating a position that might not be popular while remaining connected and engaged in the coaching dynamic, even when there is conflict.

Coaching Behaviors

Any behavior that supports the coaching process is easy when you are not anxious and seem all but intangible when you are. Performing when it counts—when you are under pressure, confused, lack confidence—is about what you do to regain those behaviors when you lose them.

Witnessing

One of the most important skills a coach has, and they undergo significant training for this, is the ability to maintain their own experience in the presence of others' anxiety. Self-differentiation sits squarely in the middle of taking a firm stand on our own point of view (our judgment, our decision, or a boundary we set), and remaining connected and attuned to those with whom we take a stand.

It's sort of like a gyroscope, where all the parts tilt, move and roll, but the center remains firm. Applying this metaphor to our relationships, we maintain an *interactional equilibrium*: the ability to maintain yourself and your relationships in the face of forces like fear, conflict, judgment, and anxiety.

Coaching without a high degree of self-differentiation can lead to a high degree of reactivity where the coach and the client can lose their balance, responding in automatic, nonconstructive and ineffective ways.

The power of the witness

It's easy to look at someone else's decisions and pass judgement. Coaches with a grounding in psychology get trained *not* to judge and to remain separate yet connected as they intervene with a client on a challenge. Curiosity, genuine nonjudgmental interest, is a quality that needs to be constantly cultivated and practiced.

"

Any behavior that supports the coaching process is easy when you are not anxious and seem all but intangible when you are.

The witness sees the good, the bad, the terrible, and the mundane. Witnessing a family member, friend, partner or associate's experience gives it meaning. *How* we witness one another's experience makes that experience constructive and positive, or devastating and painful.

In our families and at our work, we hide most of who we really are. There is more than enough judgment to go around and we can almost feel our knuckles being rapped when we play outside the lines. We know how quickly we'd be kicked from the campfire if people could read a tickertape of our mind.

Much of our inner monologue might seem foolish: how we felt a strange impulse to burst into tears during a touching commercial of family reconnection; how often we wish we could travel back in time and correct the missed opportunities of our youth, or even just take back what we said to a colleague in our last meeting. Using a harsh lens, some of what is inside can be pretty pitiful: how worried we are about asking a stupid question; how needy we feel for the attention of someone in our group; how much we worry about our appearance. There is also a part of our mind designated for the illegal. This is where the death wishes hang out—our fantasies about a work colleague, or our very plain plans for what we would like to do to a bad boss. But some of what have to contend with is substantial, as we reckon with the vulnerability we feel in undertaking scope with which we have little experience or initial understanding, like leading a team, a division, or a whole company.

When we are under stress, our thinking becomes myopic. We return to what we know works and that knowledge turns into our most powerful hammer. The problem is, not every challenge requires a hammer and our coach can help us acquire a broader perspective so that we can see and learn to develop new tools for the problems that confront us.

Not everyone knows when they need a helping hand. When our world becomes small, we are often counseled to reach out to friends and colleagues (and sometimes coaches!). But we know, deep down, that the social contract in our relationships dictates that we do not burden them with more than a mere fraction of our insanity. There is only so much, we think, we should tell a friend, colleague, or boss before we appear weak, damaged, or put ourselves at risk for being sidelined. All this contributes to our sense of feeling like an imposter, a fraud, or generally undeserving of what we have genuinely earned.

As a safety measure, we filter ourselves. In every interaction, we ensure that there remains a wall between what we say to people and what is truly going on inside our minds.

An exception lies with coaching. Here, remarkably, we can say pretty much anything we want—and expect it to remain confidential. We don't have to impress the coach or reassure them of our sanity in a particular situation or confirm the insanity in which we operate. We need to be up front, candid, and tell them what is going on. There is no need to stop them thinking we are not completely qualified to do what we do, not worthy of our roles, or just plain terrified. We can gingerly hint that we have some qualities we wish to work on, those shadows in the dark corners of our minds. And, we will find that the coach is not horrified, offended or surprised—only calmly curious. We will learn that we are not frauds, imposters, or undeserving of success. Eventually, we arrive at the opposite of isolation.

A good witness, someone grounded in a science of inquiry, is a model to us on how to become our own advocate.

Proximity

Coaches know a lot about the unembellished truths of human nature and have a broader view of what it means to be normal. They have close-up experience, proximity, working with people who have experienced serious traumas—harassment, layoffs, discrimination—as well as the smaller pains and paradoxes: a

"

Coaches know a lot about the unembellished truths of human nature and have a broader view of what it means to be normal.

grudge provoked by a side look at a person in a meeting that took up the better part of three years; an otherwise amiable person who punched a wall in frustration after a meeting; a smart, capable manager who is no longer performing well or feels stuck; a senior director in midlife at the same level for ten years and getting anxious about retirement; a general manager dealing with self-sabotage and severe reputational damage; a corporate vice president incapable of confrontation.

Because of their orientation, coaches grounded in psychology know that inside every adult there are feelings of confusion, anger, frustration, anxiety and longing to have their say and their reality recognized. Coaches appreciate that we need to know what we know and feel what we feel in order to really know ourselves again. They know we will want to be heard, perhaps through tears or the clenched jaw of frustration, which might be at odds with the surface maturity and self-management normally associated with executives and high performing managers.

Coaches understand what people are like, and how they operate. Therefore, they do not to need to censor or deliver judgments. This experience does not come from theory or books, but by being courageous about knowing their own nature. Coaches may not share our fantasies and anxieties *exactly*, but they accept that their own are as colorful and as complex as ours. They are just as well acquainted with the powerful and peculiar fears that hold us all hostage.

Coaches can start to help us because they have a much broader view of what is actually normal versus what we insist on pretending is normal. They have perspective at a time when we probably do not. They don't require us to be any particular way to protect their fragile sense of self or of reality. Their only requirement is that we admit, without too much defensiveness, to some of what is going on inside us. They ask us to feel what we might have been avoiding or know what we might have been lying to ourselves about in the pursuit of greater self-awareness. Greater self-awareness leads to deeper insights. Deeper insights leads to clearer thinking. When we think more clearly, we can start to take meaningful action.

Supportive

Finding direction for ourselves and/or leading others, at any level, isn't easy. It's an invitation into an uncomfortable place filled with doubt, constraints, difficulty, and struggle. When we accept that invitation, we find within ourselves truth, strength, and resilience.

Coaches enter into an ecosystem and understand our position in that system; they do not take on the stresses of our system. They do not prescribe what we should do. They share our concerns, convey empathy with our situation, and help us think creatively about our options. When we are stuck, or performing poorly, thinking creatively is where we are most challenged. Under pressure, we develop a myopic view of what is possible, making most options impossible.

Coaches help us identify our anxieties. They help us better understand mental processes that hold us back, keep us stuck, and inhibit our ability solve problems under pressure. Here, coaches model the behavior we are looking for: *to remain independent thinkers while working interdependently to confront challenges constructively*.

As important as self-awareness is, coaches are not there simply for understanding and insights. They demand our willingness to enter into a maturing process that helps increase our resiliency. They require us to take action, learn from our experiences, and set new goals for action that lead to a stronger sense of our leadership presence. The stronger and more robust our presence is—our ability to sit with our own discomfort and the discomfort of others—the easier it will be to integrate practicing the ability to identify reasonable goals, manage ourselves amidst our own discomfort and that of others, increase our tolerance for reactivity, and be candid with our experiences. Mastery of these practices is a lifelong commitment.

In perceiving and reacting to our performance, those around us may be sporadically annoyed, frustrated, jealous, bored, vindictive, keen to prove a point or distracted by their own set of concerns. Coaches bring a focused, generous attention to our situation. They create a safe, no-consequences conversational space, separate from day-to-day pressures. They are genuinely sorry if we have lost political capital on a project for which we bled. They understand that it must have been worrying to get a new boss right before they were promised a promotion, enraging to be overlooked after delivering a key project, or exciting to have acquired a new team. They know what it feels like to be stuck without a sense of direction. They recognize we didn't do whatever it is we are there to discuss on purpose and assume some logic on our part if we did. They do not flatter us, but they do strive to enter into our experience, shoulder to shoulder, and help us make sense of our experience so that we can see a broader set of choices than the one we originally picked. They look at reality through our eyes so as to start offering an alternative point of view and become an effective sounding board for future decision making.

Such support allows us to exhale and breathe a sigh of relief. Day to day survival in corporate politics (and everywhere else) requires that we constantly weigh the impact of our words and actions on others. We have to consider their priorities, take a genuine interest in their lives, and make room for their concerns.

With a coach, there is little inquiry into their personal experience. The coach inquires what is top of mind for us, not the other way around. The relationship is as one-sided as the parent-advocate who doesn't expect the child to worry about their sleep, but who provides ground rules to live by.

However, the coach does not sacrifice equality in the relationship. They'll show us understanding while holding us accountable to our goals. They give us tough feedback so we can see reality with greater clarity. They are fully present to help us find what is best for us, understood on our terms.

Support is not just pleasant. Support is structured, and essential to us tapping into our own reserves. Knowing that we have someone in our corner is designed to lend us the courage to face up to experiences we normally avoid. In a sufficiently calm, reassuring and attentive environment, we can look at areas of vulnerability we otherwise lack the courage to tackle. We need to learn to confront our managers unproductive interventions that derail project priorities. We need to make key leadership decisions resulting in team restructuring and strategy shifts. We have to be able to deal with toxic team members in a way that doesn't blow back on us. Above all, we must know where we are headed on our own life path, and why. With a supportive advocate in our corner, we can summon the vulnerability needed to reflect on our own decisions and behavior—that perhaps we were wrong correcting someone in front of the team, or that we made a hasty career decision that cost us, or that we have been angry with a peer for long enough, that it might be best to outgrow our justifications.

The support of another person gives us the emotional safety needed to shine light in a constructive way at our crafty, mysterious, evasive minds.

Listening

One of the structural flaws of our minds is that it is hard for us to think deeply and coherently for any length of time. We keep losing the main thread the same way we lose our keys on the way out the door. Competing, irrelevant information has a habit of darting across the mental horizon and jumbling our shaky insights. Occasionally, consciousness mysteriously goes blank for a moment, like we've lost our streaming connection. These mental glitches distract our attention, chipping away at our potential for finding creative flow in our work, and reinforce doubt in the value of what we are trying to make sense of.

"Why am I doing this? Why did I embark on this effort in the first place?" we think.

When this kind of thinking happens, we can experience overpowering urges to check the news, social media, gossip, walk around the office to distract others or search out a snack. All unproductive behaviors. All behaviors with external focus. As a result, some of the topics we most need to examine—our inner state, our interpersonal relationships; our goals; our skill development; the triggers that bother us so much about the way our colleagues do or don't do their work—sink into to the mental sands, at great mental cost.

What helps in our attempts to know our own minds is, surprisingly, having another mind present. For all the appeal of independent learning, thinking usually happens best in tandem. The curiosity of someone else gives use the confidence to remain curious about the things we are most intimidated to confront about ourselves, the dogs in the basements of our minds. It is the application of a light pressure from outside us that helps give structure and perspective to some of our jumbled impressions. That coaches require us to verbalize our thoughts mobilizes us toward greater discipline in our concentration.

Occasionally a friend might be unusually attentive and ready to hear us out. But it isn't enough for them quietly sip their coffee or cocktail and hear us out. Listening means more than merely not interrupting. To really be heard means being the recipient of a strategy of 'active listening'.

From the start, the coach will use a succession of very quiet but significant prompts to help us develop and stick to the points we are circling. These suggest that there is no hurry but that someone is there, following every word we say, sigh we take, and flinch of our voice and posture as they encourage us to "go on" and "say more."

One flower, one gardener

When someone is listening to us actively, our ideas, memories and concerns don't have to be well-formed. We are given a wide birth to stumble, backtrack, and get confused. But the active listener contains and gardens the emerging confusion. They can see the difference between a weed that will distract us and the seed that we need to learn to nurture. They help us plough old ground covered too quickly prompting us to address a relevant point that we might have skipped. They will help us chop away at a disturbing issue while continually reassuring us that what we are saying is valuable. All the while, they will note minor changes in our facial expressions, tone of voice, breathing, posture, and eye movements. They will be interested in what words we choose, and attentive not only to what we actually express but what we might have said instead.

They do not treat us like ineffective communicators; they are simply immensely alive to how difficult it is for anyone to piece together our blind spots.

Interruption

Coaches actively listen, but they also interrupt—strategically. They seek to understand—for their own sake—following their curiosity about decisions, behaviors, assumptions we are making. These decisions, behaviors, assumptions may or may not be informed by our past, but our reactivity about them most certainly is.

We come to coaching with certain goals. We are seeking answers. There is a presenting problem that hints at, but does not fully capture, the full picture. Why, for instance, do we repeatedly hire people who do not perform? Why do we seek out bosses that do not support us? Why is it so hard for us to work through others? How can we be both so convinced we need to leave a role and yet have remained completely unable to find something more fulfilling? Why do we sabotage our potential?

By their questions and their attention, the coach tries—harder than anyone we've spoken to yet—to discover how our presenting problem connects to something larger. In particular, they help us navigate "the systems web": ourselves and our team(s); our wider ecosystem of departments, vendors, customers, and strategic stakeholders or partners; and, how we interpret "the outside" market, the economy, the natural environment, and political shifts (as appropriate). Remember, the coach's goal is to help us increase effectiveness by interweaving relationships with results, pinpointing key areas of growth.

Starting in the first session, we gather a succession of small discoveries with the coach to contribute to an emerging picture of the sources of our presenting problem, not just the symptoms.

When we view ourselves at the center of our systems web, we gain insights in the way in which our character has slowly evolved in response to early wounds. We learn how those wounds form into triggers, and how our reactivity to those triggers hampers our possibilities today.

Reactivity narrows our focus. Responsiveness broadens our view. In the space between reactivity and response is where we find the seeds of our creativity.

When we view ourselves interacting with our teams and wider ecosystems, these triggers amplify. Do we trust others enough to delegate? Can we get past our initial judgments of peers enough to collaborate effectively rather than work around them? Can we learn to engage rather than avoid difficult personalities we encounter as managers, partners or stakeholders?

When we take in the even broader environments (social systems, market competition, etc.) we notice additional pressures in the system.

We may, for example, start to sense how a feeling of rivalry with another manager led us to take on more challenges to compete for a boss's approval, as well as seeing, perhaps for the first time, that the logic of our self-sabotage no longer holds. Or we might perceive the way an attitude of negativity and pessimism, which restricts our personalities and our friendships, might have had its origins in a someone who let us down at a time when we could not contain our vulnerability, and thereby turned us into people who try at every juncture to disappoint themselves early and definitively rather than allowing the world to mock our emerging hopes at a time of its own choosing.

It is unhelpful to state any of this too frankly, to any client, as they are likely to resist. There is a dance to active listening—and not everyone is dancing to the same music. There are useful or counterproductive behaviors that we can have with our coach. Here are some examples (the first two are constructive, the second two are less effective):

- we want advice, the coach fosters independent thinking.

- we seek feedback, the coach gives it.

- we vent about a colleague, coach soothes.

- we are late for appointments or forget to reserve a room, the coach tolerates it.

Often, the dance pattern developing between you and your coach is an example of the system the client is in with their own team or organization. Systems have a way of extending themselves out to their furthest boundaries. In that way, they have a strong gravitational pull.

The coach resists this by reflecting to us the decisions we are making, or how we are reacting and behaving. Together, we replay those scenarios and discuss alternatives. For the process to work, the coach reflects of the structure of our troubles in a way we can best interpret it as our own observation and insight.

A partnership

The ongoing contact we have with a coach, the sessions that may last one month, or continue less sporadically over years, contribute to the creation of a partnership. Our coach is a partner in our success and personal and professional mastery of being able to: create, make progress toward, and maintain reasonable goals; manage ourselves amidst our own discomfort and that of others; increase our tolerance for reactivity; and be candid with our experiences. Because these skills are hard for everyone, mastery takes a lifetime. A coach is there for part of that journey.

We are almost certain to have approached a coach in the first place because, in some way, partnering has become fraught with challenges. We sense the issues, but don't quite understand the root of the problem. Maybe we try to please too many people. We gain our sense of security from their admiration, but then feel inauthentic or inwardly numb and pull back. Perhaps we connect strongly at first with a direct, boss, or stakeholder, but then always discover a major flaw that turns us off and baits us to sabotage the relationship by avoiding contact or withholding information that will make them successful, establishing an unproductive cycle.

The relationship with our coach may have little in common with the sort of partnerships we have elsewhere in our life. Because therapists spend so much time in a client's past, they remove all potential for collegial rapport. Because coaches focus so much on the present, and partner on strategies for gaining results in the present—this relationship has a bit of latitude. Some coaches do socialize with their clients; others draw a bright line. Coaches experience a conflict when a private or personal interest appears to influence the objective of his or her official duties as a coach and a professional. When that happens, they openly disclose any such conflict and offer to remove themselves when a conflict arises.

Regardless, unavoidably and conveniently, we bring to our coaching partnership the very tendencies that emerge in our relationships with other people across our systems web. Here too we may be too quick to bond thinking we have found the safety of a "tribe", only to cool, or we are too prone to idealization placing the coach upon a pedestal, then gripped by an impulse to flee.

Except that now, when we are with our coach, our tendencies will have a chance to be witnessed, slowed down, discussed, sympathetically explored and—in their more sabotaging displays— overcome. The relationship with the coach becomes a barometer of one's behavior with people more generally and thereby allows us, on the basis of greater self-awareness, to modify and improve how we relate to ourselves, our teams and stakeholders, and the world at large.

In the context of a coaching session, our biases, idiosyncrasies, beliefs, and habits are observed and can be commented on. We are not criticized, but we are held accountable. The coach notices important information about our character that we deserve to become aware of. The coach will (kindly) point out that we're reacting as if we had been attacked, when they only asked a question. The coach might focus our attention to how we seem to want to tell them impressive things about our accomplishments for the week (yet they like us anyway). The coach might notice how we seem to rush to agree with them when they're only exploring an idea to see if it fits our situation and one in which they themselves are not very sure. They see where we adopt attitudes or outlooks that we don't actually have. They see how committed we seem to be in the idea that they are disappointed in us for our lack of progress or inability to perform under pressure as we might have liked. They will point out our habit of casting people in the present in roles that must derive from the past and will search with us for the origins of these attributions, which are liable to mimic

"

The coaching relationship acts as a microcosm of our relationships in general.

what we felt towards influential caregivers and now shape what we expect from everyone.

The coaching relationship acts as a microcosm of our relationships in general. It makes a unique vehicle for learning about our less noticeable emotional and behavioral tendencies. By re-experiencing relational problems with another person who will not respond as ordinary people will, who will not shout at us, fire us, complain, say nothing or run away, we can be helped to understand what we are up to and given a chance to let new patterns of relating emerge which help us achieve the results we are after.

The partnership with the coach becomes a template for how we might collaborate with others going forward, freed from the maneuvers and background assumptions that we carried within us from childhood, and that can impede us so grievously in the present.

The coaching partnership may be for us the first properly healthy collaboration we have had. We learn to hold off from imposing our assumptions on the other and trust them enough to let them see the larger, more complex reality of who we are—we allow ourselves to be vulnerable as we learn as we manage anxiety, frustration or embarrassment. It becomes a model—earned in a highly unusual situation—that we start to apply in the more mundane aspects of our lives, with our colleagues, bosses, stakeholders, and further aspects of our systems web.

Our Inner Voices

Somewhere in our minds, removed from the day to day, there sits a judge. They watch what we do, study how we perform, examine the effect we have on others, track our successes and failures—and then, eventually, they pass a verdict. The origins of the voice of the inner judge is simple to trace: it is the internalization of the voice of people who were once outside of us. We absorb the tones of contempt and indifference or of charity and warmth that we will have heard across our formative years. Sometimes, a voice is positive and benign, encouraging us to run those final few yards. More often, the inner voice is not nice at all. It is defeatist and punitive, panic-ridden and humiliating. It does not represent anything like our best insights or most mature capacities.

Part of what coaching offers us is a chance to improve how we judge ourselves and the voices we hear in our heads. It can involve learning—in a conscious, deliberate way—to speak to ourselves in a way the coach spoke to us over many months. In the face of challenges, we can enquire of ourselves, 'And what would they say now?' After we have heard their constructive, supportive voice often enough, and around enough tricky issues, our new response will become naturally more supportive. Eventually, our inner voice will become less judgmental and more constructive when we're trying to perform under pressure.

Chapter Reflections

Every coach brings different skills and experience to the table. What qualities, skills, and experience do you imagine your ideal coach possessing, and how has this changed after learning more about the coach-client partnership?

A system is like a spider web, where the action of one person can impact the experience and potential reactions of everyone or thing else within that web—how does that metaphor resonate with you, and how do you function in your own system/web?

Which of the coaching behaviors that you've learned about so far resonates most with your current needs? Why those a this particular time?

4

CASE STUDIES

One of the best ways to understand what coaching involves is to read accounts of what happened to people when they went: the problems they came in with, the discussions that were had, and how things changed as a result. What follows are three representative case studies of the coaching process: one individual challenge, one team challenge, and one organizational challenge.

Each case presents multiple variables to assess and consider but will be used to illustrate a central concept. Also, there are dynamics between the coach and client that I will not delve into as this is not a handbook on how to coach but rather a resource to gain a high-level understanding of how coaching works and benefits us.

The names presented here are not the names of actual clients and details have been changed to protect anonymity.

Individual Challenge

Brian. Director leading a cross-functional team of 40 located across two regions (New York, San Francisco).

Presenting issue(s): interpersonal conflict (with specific person), sleep loss, high anxiety.

> *"I've been at the company four years in good standing and on the rise. Recently, I was recently promoted to a*

> *management role. My scope of responsibility and team increased by 50%. I have a good relationship with my manager. While he doesn't provide very instructional feedback, I value his ability to objectively analyze a situation.*
>
> *I've worked hard to achieve harmony and high-performance on my team. As part of my scope increase, I inherited an extremely disruptive engineer and I need strategies on how to manage him more effectively while I move the rest of the group forward."*

Starting with the question of *"where will Anxiety appear today?"* never fails to provide initial direction for both client and coach. Anxiety is an early-warning device that alerts the system to counter with some sort of coping mechanism, often some form of fight or flight. All organisms—even the amoebic—react to stimulus they perceive to be dangerous. Courage is learning how to *respond*.

In this case, the client's lopsidedness showed itself in his dynamic with an employee joining his team. The client, Brian, is thrown off balance by his own reactivity. Others witnessing his reactivity were also thrown off balance. These are the rippling effects behavior can have.

As a result, Brian's thinking became narrow. His creativity in thinking through solutions and alternative responses to dealing with the new team member, whom we'll name Chuck, went down. Instead of successfully navigating around barriers, both Brian and Chuck became stuck and felt vulnerable.

Key Concept: Anxiety Triangles

At the center of our systems web, we sit with our challenges and opportunities. Sometimes we can manage the pressure as we negotiate the space in between. Other times we seek relief. A common challenge at the individual level is managing anxiety. Feelings of

"

Starting with the question of *"where will Anxiety appear today?"* **never fails to provide initial direction for both client and coach.**

inadequacy, incompetence, and frustration—among others—can take us farther from gaining a feel for our work.

In low stress situations, talented leaders with low anxiety meet most challenges well and can accomplish two primary aspects of leadership: 1) take clear stands on issues, while at the same time 2) remaining connected to the people who report to them. This looks something like the diagram below.

When pressures intensify, and the leader's reactivity to the challenge escalates, more internal tension is created. Anxiety reaches a level where the person is flooded with emotion (frustration, fear, anger, irritation, boredom, disappointment, sadness, etc.).

When someone is flooded, their normal responses are overwhelmed, reducing their ability to take clear positions, make thoughtful decisions, stay connected to the team, or both. Anxiety looks something like this diagram.

Now we have a distinction between a "clear" connection with challenge, and a connection that contains some level of "static." How do we determine if Brian is falling into reactivity versus a response? There is a strong cocktail of thoughts, feelings, and desires that sound something like:

- "I don't know what to do now."

- "Can't he just do what I need him to do."

- "I can no longer determine what I need to do first, when it comes to this particular issue."

- "If he knew what I was really up against, he'd stop being so difficult."

- "I'm looking for a single-answer solution (move him out of the group, fire him, etc.)."

- "I'm alone in this."

- "I've been let down. How did this person make it this far in the organization? Why do I always have to step up and take care of things?"

These sentiments are a few of many examples of someone in the throes of reactive thinking. When we are overwhelmed, we lose connection to our inner resolve and resilience. These kinds of statements hint at a client's disconnection from themselves (due to overwhelm).

Triangles: Who Owns The Anxiety?

Anxiety, like any feeling, is comprised of energy. It can move through us and around a room faster than a brush fire. When we face anxiety our first response is to seek an outlet to relieve ourselves of this feeling. There are healthy, constructive triangles and there are unhealthy, unconstructive triangles. Seeking guidance from a manager, mentor or coach is constructive. Gossiping to peers is unconstructive.

"

Anxiety,
like any feeling,
is comprised
of energy.
It can move
through us
and around
a room faster
than a
brush fire.

Here are a few examples of triangles we have likely experienced in our lives:

ANXIOUS PERSON	FEELS PRESSURE FROM	TURNS TO
wife	partner	work
child	teacher	parent
husband	partner	gym
employee	manager	human resources
customer	customer service rep	sales
customer	shop mechanic	local dealer
vendor	warehouse manager	production manager

Individuals form triangles under stress. And, we scan for stress every five seconds. So, we are always in a triangle for some reason or other. Brian, the senior director is anxious because he feels challenged by Chuck, an engineer he has inherited as part of a reorganization. Chuck was against the reorg and believes himself to be Brian's peer.

Chuck is engaging in toxic gossip to undermine Brian, and not doing his work. Brian is disturbed about the relationship he has with Chuck and the new demands of his role. To relieve his anxiety, Brian turns to his manager who recommends he speak with a coach.

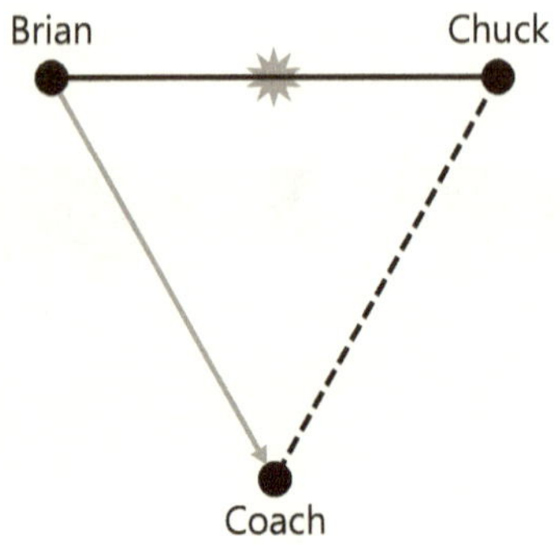

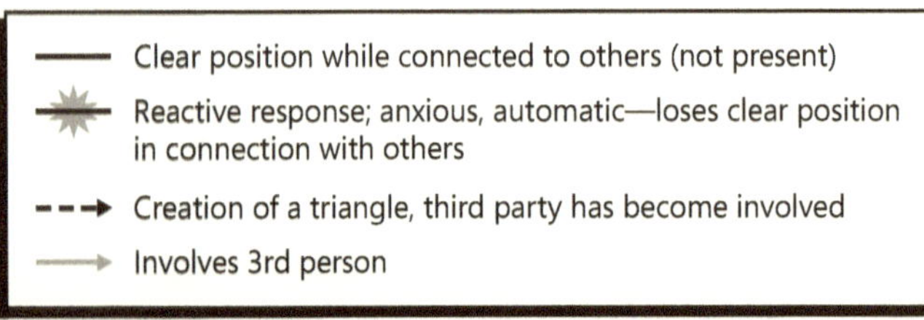

Brian could triangle others into his relationship with Chuck constructively and unconstructively. Some possibilities include:

- Brian could vent to one of his directs about Chuck. He might leave a meeting shaking his head: "Can you believe the lack of accountability Chuck had in that meeting? He thinks he has a shot at getting promoted!"

- Brian could create an alliance with a peer by turning them against Chuck. He says to his peer: "I worked with Chuck in the past and never experienced the kind of attitude and lack of responsibility he's displayed in this role. He's smart, but in the long run, I'm not sure this environment is the best fit for him."

- Brian could go to human resources (HR) and to help Chuck become more effective working with others and being more effective in his role: "Chuck lacks accountability needed at his level in the organization. Can you help him find a coaching resource so he can benefit from feedback from others in his group as well as his stakeholders? We've gone back and forth on this issue and we're not getting anywhere."

Sound familiar? The first two examples illustrate how we can react to anxiety and try to cast it off onto someone else, get rid of it, pass it on to someone else to process, or even hide from it. Not very effective. The anxiety is still present and unresolved. The real challenge is finding the courage to confront the situation directly and discover what is required from him as a leader, align it to the business's needs and determine a considered response.

Distraction By Triangle

When leaders react, it causes ripples of reaction in other parts of the organization. Reactivity can show up in requests, rules, policies, demands, or gossip. Reactions tend to drain a system of energy and creative problem-solving. Here is what happens with Brian.

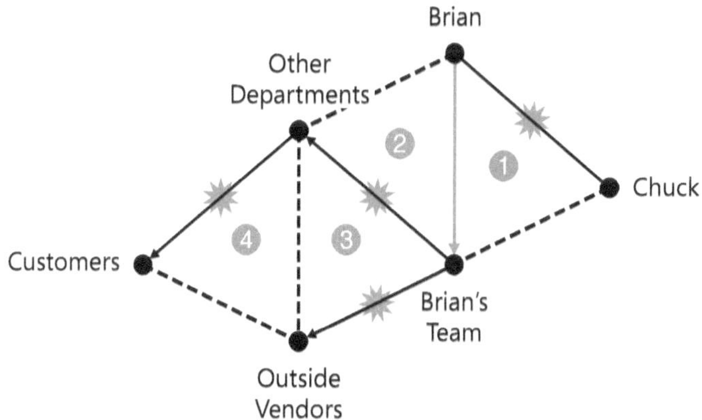

Before speaking with his coach, Brian, vents within his directs' team. Chuck has already been spreading gossip so some of this venting feels like it's attempting to tap down small fires. Brian eludes to Chuck as challenging to hold to account—something everyone feels (triangle 1). Brian's team has also seen this behavior and is generally upset about the reorg; they didn't want this team in the first place and feels like the group is growing too quickly. They sympathize with Brian and acknowledge several challenges Brian is facing given his visibility to the CEO. After the meeting, the different groups engage in the gossip grapevine. It feeds the team's anxiety about their own sense of job security. Gossip also ignites resentment about having to change technology platforms and increases speculation that Brian could do more to toe the line with Chuck (and potentially others).

How A Coach Can Help

A coach's primary goal in helping Brian is to engage in forming a healthy triangle. Giving Brian's anxiety a no-consequence area to hang out while he thinks through what to do helps Brian understand and confront his own reactions. With space to untangle himself from his circumstances, he can get back to a neutral equilibrium and engage his innate creativity in thinking through solutions.

Team Challenge

Mark. Director leading a cross-functional team of six located across three regions (Seattle, London, San Francisco).

Presenting issue(s): low management scores, particularly in developing others, trust, and transparency. Negative feedback on the manager internally (among team and external stakeholders) and externally (e.g., Glassdoor, etc.).

> *"I've been at the company two years in good standing. Recently, I was promoted to a management role. It was significantly more complicated than I understood it to be. I have a supportive manager, but rarely get concrete direction or feedback from him on what I*

"

It's one thing to get a client's account of their leadership challenges, but it's quite another to see it in action.

need to do. My management scores tanked this last year; I was viciously talked about on the app, Blind; and, I feel overwhelmed and like I'm in a nosedive I can't get out of."

In this case, the client's inability to manage group dynamics led to focusing on two primary aspects of how he led meetings. The client, whom we'll name Mark, needed to get: 1) more constructive feedback from his manager, 2) more input from directs and stakeholders that up-leveled the quality of discussions and 2) better definition in his decisions. He contracted to work with his coach for live team coaching at his meetings to help him and his team improve in these areas.

Key Concept: Pattern Breaking In Real Time

It's one thing to get a client's account of their leadership challenges, but it's quite another to see it in action. Observation of clients and live-action coaching gives coaches a deeper sense of the reinforcing patterns that clients and their teams contribute while sharing space in the systems web. It is, in many respects, just-in-time, on-the-job training and guidance of the client when it counts the most.

The coach looks for opportunities to change a client's ineffective patterns, in real time. Let's look at the situation of Mark's struggle to manage both up and down effectively. He and I spent some time planning and looking at his side of the unsuccessful pattern. By looking at the gaps in sponsorship from his manager, the vice-president of engineering, he could lift one of his directs out of firefighting situations and help prioritize the team's roadmap and backlog (two tasks that had been bogging him down).

Mark was now ready to address his own contribution to the ineffective pattern with his team as a unit. At the beginning of each meeting, Mark let everyone know not only the agenda for the meeting, but what he wanted to work on and why I was there to help him.

I had coached Mark to add one more thing: if anyone noticed him straying from these goals, they should speak up and mention it rather than wait for me to intervene. This gives some of the responsibility to the team for making sure the meeting is run well. After all, the team is always there, I am not. Building self-sufficiency from the start reduces reliance on outside coaches.

Mark, and each of his team members, contracted to initiate behaviors that Mark wanted to see and attain the goals each had identified to improve their individual effectiveness in meetings.

Watching this group in action, however, I witnessed the group continually losing track of the conversation. Decisions were not clear, which impacted the clarity of roles and overall ownership. Just fifteen minutes into the meeting and the conversation was disjointed, tangential, and unproductive. Either Mark didn't notice or made no attempt to get the meeting back on track. When he took up a topic leading toward a rabbit hole, I intervened, "Mark, the meeting is covering a wide array of topics, what would be most helpful to decide upon right now?"

Over the course of the conversation, I intervened in several other ways:

To Mark: "A decision was just made, but I don't think all the team members have clarity on what it was. Can you reiterate it so everyone is on the same page?"

To the Team: "The goal that was stated earlier is to hear from everyone. You can help Mark make sure that happens either by inviting comments from those who haven't spoken or speaking up if you haven't weighed in yet."

To Mark: "Are you ready to move on, or do you want to hear from more people?"

To a specific team member: "To help you achieve your individual goal of speaking up and influencing, now would be the time to show your peer you understand what she just said before giving your opinion."

My interventions above—to Mark, the team, to individuals— helps keep the people accountable to the conversation they want to have. It takes the confident vulnerability of a leader to invite constructive feedback on how they can become more effective, as well as each person doing their own part in living their vision for a successful interaction. In this case, that meant hearing from everyone.

Chapter Reflections

Two concepts, triangles and pattern breaking, were illustrated by case studies. How have you experienced these ideas in your career? What part have you played?

How would you like to adjust the role you play in your current system?

CONCLUSION

Our Suspicions Of Coaching

It is easy to be suspicious of coaching. Three common myths of coaching are, it: is reserved for poor performers, is a self-indulgent activity, and will change everything.

Coaching Is For Poor Performers, Or The Broken.

A common myth of coaching is that it is a resource reserved for employees at risk or in need of "being fixed." Only when we are drastically failing at our jobs, we think, would we ever consider asking someone for help.

But coaching is simply a mature response to very normal anxieties of the workplace. Everyone reckons with frustration, anxiety, or overwhelm. Those emotions are the inevitable result of having taken on a large scope of work with little training, support, or development—a common experience. When we are under pressure, we develop coping strategies—of which we lack awareness—that hurt or sabotage us and others and limit our capacities for contentment. In this specific sense, we are all frustrated, anxious, and overwhelmed and, therefore, prime candidates for help of some kind. What qualifies us for coaching is not a major catastrophe in our careers; it is enough that we are simply human.

Coaching Is Self-indulgent.

It is tempting to state something a 'luxury' when we know little of it. Depending on your point of view, it can be considered a 'luxury' to read all the time, exercise every day, bake bread instead of buying it. The term 'luxury' is simply an insult for what one has no interest in rather than a category defined by cost.

Coaching is routinely perceived as being self-indulgent. The concern is that by talking intimately about ourselves once a week or more, our personalities are at risk of growing dangerously self-absorbed. The interest of coaching may, the assumption goes, cause a belief that we can and should find moments of our work history as compelling as they proved in a coaching session. But this is to misunderstand the origins of the ego, which lies not in excessive intelligent attention but neglect. Coaching is unlikely to make us less interested in the lives and work of others; the higher probability is that it will free us from our inner suffering, that to date prevented us from participating fully in the experiences of those around us.

Another worry is that coaching is a costly replacement for a more effective manager, and indicates a failure to develop the patience, empathy, and systems perspective involved in cultivating a healthy manager-direct dynamic. But this defense of the healthy manager relationship fails to acknowledge the rules and codes of conduct that govern the institution. We cannot expect an ordinary man-ager to listen with specific knowledge, care, and persistence every week to our ongoing troubles. We cannot assume they will put their own needs to one side while linking and making sense of our lifelong patterns. These assumptions would be ambitious. Unique insights require unique professional skills. It's a lot like wishing a friend to perform open-heart surgery on us because they like us.

It is appropriately respectful of the manager dynamic to know all that it cannot be and do.

Coaching Will Change Everything.

The last but most crucial coaching myth is that coaching over-promises. It can, unwisely, be presented as the key to transforming us into rich, invincible achievers at home and work. Such inflated promises rightly invite doubt. But ultimately, they are not a true reflection of what coaching hopes to do for us. Its real aim is more limited: to assist us in the task of becoming slightly more mature, somewhat less reactionary, and to be a more self-aware participant in their professional drama. Coaching cannot cancel out the essential wrinkles of misunderstanding between coworkers or quell the rumor mill of an organization. Still, it can equip us to cope with these circumstances with more insight, courage, and confidence.

How Coaching Might Change Us

Who are we after coaching, if the process were to go as well as could be hoped?

We will still be learning. People will continue to misunderstand us; we will meet with opposition; there will still be goals that will be out of reach; success will come to people who don't appear to deserve it. There will be qualities we have that will still not be fully appreciated by others. We will still have to compete with and submit to the judgment of those around us; we will still be too far in or too far out of organizational politics—trying to strike the right balance. Coaching doesn't make our lives or careers better than they truly are.

"

Who are we after coaching, if the process were to go as well as could be hoped?

However, with these caveats in place, coaching can still bring substantial benefits.

1. **We will have slightly more freedom**

   The coping beliefs and behaviors we choose to protect our primal wound are rigid. We develop fixed mindsets about people and circumstances and that limits our room for movement and development. For example, we may seek a distinctive personality type for a boss; or we gravitate toward certain peers; or we avoid developing certain skills (like public speaking); or, we have to be constantly cynical or else insistently perky (both alienating behaviors). Our sense of who we can be and what we can do is held prisoner by past experiences. Coaching can liberate us from these patterns by helping to increase self-awareness around such patterns and inclinations.

2. **We learn to take a stand and advocate, for ourselves, first—then others.**

   With one leader we were humiliated and silent. With another we felt defensive and combative. But experiencing a coach's patience, kindness, and attention encourages us to be less frustrated with ourselves. A coach's constructive reflections of our reactivity help us gain awareness and clarity of our core needs. Having once voiced our deeper fears and wishes for our careers with a coach, we can bring those goals or stand our ground again with someone else. We learn there may be an alternative to silence, frustration, and remaining stuck in our ways.

   With a greater sense of our right to speak up, we may become more aware and better at articulating our particularly unique contributions and perspective. Instead of just resenting another person's criticism and quickly falling on our sword, we might explain why they perceive us the way they do. If we are upset by our boss or peers, we don't need

"

Those that have wounded or slighted us almost invariably didn't mean to do so...

to accuse them of evil and leave the room or fantasize about quitting. Rather than seeking various forms of escape, we now know how to explain our sensitivities to certain criticism and what support we need to feel "safe enough" on the team to contribute. Instead of trying to pretend that nothing is ever our fault, we can offer a candid explanation or our limitations and commit to trying to do better going forward. Only when we learn to advocate effectively for ourselves can we start to advocate effectively for others.

3. **We can be more compassionate, with ourselves, first—then others.**

In the course of coaching, we will realize how much we were let down by certain people in the past. Former bosses or mentors might have fallen short or failed us in some way. They didn't pave the way, stick their neck out, stand up for, or develop us the way we needed. A natural response might be blame. But the eventual constructive and more mature reaction (building on an understanding of how our own flaws arose) will be to interpret the behavior of those we needed because of their own unique set of circumstances. Maybe those bosses, mentors or peers were suffering their own dramas and constraints. A coach helps us develop empathy and perspective that those that have wounded or slighted us almost invariably didn't mean to do so; they were themselves hurt and struggling to endure. And even if they did mean those actions against us, we have a choice in how we respond.

We can develop a more compassionate picture of a world in which complexities and anxieties are blindly passed down and around organizations. The insight isn't only true to experience; holding it in mind will mean there is less to fear the next time those crises come around, enabling us to make smarter more considered decisions. Only when we learn to be compassionate with ourselves can we start showing compassion for others.

In these ways, coaching will have done some of its most important work.

The ability to self-manage, see clearly, and make good decisions impacts leaders at all levels in every sector. Imagine contending with the emotional complexity we've just reviewed in this little book, while they face:

- Protecting staff, seeking support through a broken chain of command, while getting a naval warship safely to dock amidst a global pandemic;

- Deciding on the path of artificial intelligence for a social media organization while it is actively impacting a nationwide election; or

- Adapting a global retail organization from being everyone's "third place" in the community to gather and linger with their coffees to takeout only, resisting layoffs and preserving an hourly workforce.

Coaching is more relevant now than it has ever been.

Chapter Reflections

What suspicions did you have about coaching before reading this book? Do you still have suspicions?

What coaching outcomes resonated with you most? Why those at this particular time?

Acknowledgements

Compassion for self, compassion for others, are things that have to be intentionally and actively cultivated.

—Cheryl Cebula, MSW & LIOS
Systems Counseling Faculty

It has been said 'that which is shareable is bearable.' So it is that conversations in coaching create the possibility of learning how to be graceful with one's learning experience while moving creatively through life.

The seeds for this book started during my graduate school experience when I encountered a professor who, by her example, single-handedly changed the course of my career. If I attain even half of her abilities in my lifetime, I will consider myself a success. Cheryl Cebula, I hope you are looking down on me, and I thank you from the bottom of my heart for demonstrating such thorough knowledge, experience, and connection in a way that was both challenging and inspiring to me.

No work is ever done alone. There were many people who supported me through this little pocket-guide series, helping me gnash through ideas, outlines, and experiences to tell a more coherent story. Enormous thanks to Steve, whose belief in me never wavers.

There were people who offered everything from tremendous emotional support for my endeavors in providing observations, insightful questions, and challenging feedback on early versions of the work: Carol Jakus, Diane Wagner, Jan Monti, Lara Hanson, and Frances Strickland.

To John Hinds, Shelley Roberts your friendship and comments have directly influenced my overall work.

To treasured friends, you know who you are, my gratitude to you is deep and wide for the support you've given me. Our shared journey has been my great gift.

Thanks to Rob Nance for everything graphical and lovely; I've appreciated your guidance in the process.

To all the clients I've worked with who generously shared a slice of their life experiences with me: thank you for bringing this series to life. You are smart, talented, and generous. I never reference specific clients for privacy reasons—but you know who you are! It's my honor to venture into the sometimes-rough neighborhoods of your minds alongside you and to help re-frame your thoughts in a way that moves you forward. The transformations you experience continue to inspire me in helping people to first learn how to become their own best advocates. Only then, can they reach their goals and tap their innate potential.

Thank you for reading—I will be your biggest cheerleader and advocate wherever you go from here. My hope is that you develop and learn strategies that help you exceed your own expectations of yourself.

Take good care,

Christine Haskell, PhD

Resources for Individuals

Individuals looking to develop an ongoing practice for themselves might find it hard to get started. Whether you've just wrapped up a coaching engagement or looking to establish a foundation for yourself before engaging with a coach, the Coaching Toolkit can be helpful in maintaining forward momentum.

The Coaching Toolkit

Video Series

Short, single-concept video sessions reinforce several of Christine's core coaching concepts, such as levels of awareness, triggers, self-management, constructive conversations and influencing. These six sessions help you increase your knowledge of your own dynamics during performance under pressure and sustain your practice with these ideas as you continue to integrate them into your day-to-day thinking.

Materials & Templates

The Coaching Toolkit has everything you need to get started quickly, easily, and regularly with your own practice. You will get instant access to materials including template emails to help you communicate progress to your mentors and managers.

Learn more at **ChristineHaskell.com/workshops**

Online Resources

Ways To Stay In Touch?

- Questions, success stories, or feedback to share? I would love to hear from you! E-mail **hello@christinehaskell.com**

- Subscribe to **ChristineHaskell.com**, to receive the latest blog posts and updates in your inbox.

Want To Help Spread the Word?

Authors don't keep books alive; readers do. If you enjoyed a book in this series and think others could benefit, I would be grateful for your help in any of the following ways:

- Write a review on the retailer's site where you purchased the book and/or Goodreads, to help others decide whether to purchase a copy.

- Gift a copy to a friend or co-worker.

Recommended Reading

The work I do stands on the shoulders of giants. Below are books covering the major concepts in each chapter. These books provide in-depth coverage of areas I only scratched the surface. I encourage you to dig deeper into anything that grabbed you.

Coaching V Therapy

- *Co-active coaching: New skills for coaching people toward success in work and life*, L. Whitworth

- *Professional Coaching Competencies: The Complete Guide*, D. Goldvarg; P. Mathews; N. Perel (Author), J. Auerbach (Editor)

How Framing The Past Produces New Insights

- *Extraordinary relationships: a new way of thinking about human interactions*, R. Gilbert

- *Triggers: Creating Behavior That Lasts--Becoming the Person You Want to Be*, M. Goldsmith

- *The Intimacy Paradox: Personal Authority in the Family System*, D, Williamson, D. Williamson

- *The Primal Wound: Understanding the Adopted Child*, N. Verrier

- *The Body Keeps the Score: Brain, Mind, and Body in the Healing of Trauma*, by B. van der Kolk MD

- *It Didn't Start with You: How Inherited Family Trauma Shapes Who We Are and How to End the Cycle*, by M. Wolynn

- *Bowenian family systems theory: Approaches and applications.* In D. Capuzzi & M. D. Stauffer (Eds.), *Foundations of couples, marriage, and family counseling*, Kim-Appel, D., & Appel, J. K.

- *The invisible web: Gender patterns in family relationships.* M. Walters, B. Carter, P. Papp., & O. Silverstein

How Coaching Can Tend To the Present And The Future

- *Professional Coaching Competencies: The Complete Guide, Damian Goldvarg; P. Mathews*; N. Perel (Author), J. Auerbach (Editor)

- *What got you here won't get you there: How successful people become even more successful*, Marshall Goldsmith

- *Emotional Intelligence: Why It Can Matter More Than IQ*, D. Goleman

- *Mindset: The New Psychology of Success*, C. Dweck

Case Studies

- *Extraordinary relationships: a new way of thinking about human interactions*, R. Gilbert

- *Seeing Systems: Unlocking the Mysteries of Organizational Life*, B. Oshry

- *Leadership without easy answers*, R. Heifetz

- *Thanks for the feedback: the science and art of receiving feedback well (even when it is off base, unfair, poorly delivered, and, frankly, you're not in the mood)*, S. Heen, & D. Stone

- *How the Way We Talk Can Change the Way We Work: Seven Languages for Transformation.*, R. Keegan, L. Lahey

- *A Failure of Nerve: Leadership in the Age of the Quick Fix*, by E. Friedman

About the Author

Leaders must summon the courage to see what others cannot and say what needs to be said; to sit amidst their own discomfort as well as others and live with the strength that comes from both failure and success—all of which require the ability to drive results with others in the background and the foreground.

Christine Haskell, PhD is a seasoned technology veteran, leadership coach, and adjunct professor. For over twenty years, she has been at the nexus of technology and innovation, at every stage in a company's growth cycle. She has developed first-generation products (Yahoo!, RealNetworks) and lead division-wide, global programs (Microsoft, Starbucks) in both startup and established software, internet, and software-as-service companies.

As a trained social scientist, she observes patterns and makes connections between behaviors and goals. She is known for blending directness with humor and compassion. Elevating organizational capabilities and supporting systems differentiates her work. She achieves consistent results by emphasizing real business creativity in the use of systems, defining a clear and compelling ROI, and by helping both leaders and stakeholders integrate and evolve business processes.

OTHER BOOKS IN THIS SERIES

For the past several years Christine has worked with busy leaders giving them practical tools for the obstacles, conflicts, tensions that come up every day. What if managers and leaders could self-reflect, redirect their behaviors to become more effective?

Self-awareness is a foundation skill in need of intentional, active cultivation. Each book provides topic-specific tools, exercises and information to continue your growth and development.

Driving Results Through Others

There is nothing quite like learning on the job. Effective management comes with practice. Strong leadership comes by being battle-tested. When the stakes feel high and our patience runs thin, there is little room for a spirit of practice. And that is the critical moment, under pressure to perform, when leaders at all levels need to train their minds to think more effectively. This guide pulls together over 30 approaches and reflections organized against central emotional intelligence principles: self-awareness, self-regulation, empathy, motivation, and social skills. Use the guide for in-the-moment advice and perspective, or as inspiration for reflection. Summarize valuable approaches in the back of the book to comprise your own development curriculum.

Driving Change During Difficult Times

Most leaders advance initially because they are good at what they do, not necessarily because they understand people. Focusing on the processes and activities needed to complete a project will only ever get us so far. Understanding how people are affected by those processes and projects helps reduce the uncertainty that can lead to anxiety, confusion, and resistance from the people on the ground who may not fully understand the need for the changes or how to adopt and adapt to new processes. Without buy-in from the rest of the organization, a project's outcomes can fall flat. This guide pulls together over 30 approaches and reflections organized against central change management principles: awareness, desire, knowledge, ability, and reinforcement. Each concept is illustrated by common issues faced by both first-time managers and executives, as they navigate the small and large changes of their day-to-day. People applying these tools continually, will see change in how they respond versus react when the pressure is on, how they take the extra effort to cultivate empathy in order to collaborate, and how they start to advocate for themselves more constructively.

The books in this series emphasize skills we need to learn on the job, where we develop a "feel" for our work. To learn well requires the rigor of self-reflection, a commitment to critical thinking, and the development of an intentional learning practice. Each book provides reflections and a way for the reader to develop their own learning curriculum.

Theory, models, and catchphrases to "do more of this or that" just don't cut it. Reflection without purpose doesn't drive results. By practicing the tools in these books, we train our minds to perform better under pressure. We can increase the quality of our thinking to drive better decision making and bottom-line results when the stakes are high.

GIVE THIS TO SOMEONE THAT COULD BENEFIT FROM COACHING

The guides in this series are innovative, road-tested tools that can change behavior by helping people to understand the link between how people frame challenge and change in the workplace as part of a larger pattern. By slowing down to check what data they are selecting to form assumptions and codify beliefs—they can make better decisions, take more informed actions, and increase their leadership effectiveness.

"Deeply scrutinizing some of the smallest interactions with Christine led to profound insights for me about what I bring to an interaction." –**Director, Instagram**

"I tried some of Christine's suggestions with my wife first, to practice, and she immediately saw a change in how I engaged with her. I tried it with someone I was experiencing conflict with at work and it really helped." –**Senior Director, Facebook**

"Working with Christine using some of these tools has been one of the single, most impactful development activities I've engaged in." –**Senior Creative Director, Microsoft**

"Christine distills the essentials of managing and leading to short, easy to find tools and strategies that stretch your comfort zone. Choosing just a few to focus on helped me twofold. I provided more effective support to my employees and co-workers. And, I learned how to better coach myself." –**Superintendent, U.S. Naval Shipyard**

You can learn more at **www.christinehaskell.com/books** or contact Christine directly at **hello@christinehaskell.com**